THINKERS
50

Leadership

Organizational Success
Through Leadership

D0011871

STUART CRAINER + DES DEARLOVE

Mc
Graw
Hill
Education

New York   Chicago   San Francisco   Athens   London   Madrid
Mexico City   Milan   New Delhi   Singapore   Sydney   Toronto

1 2 3 4 5 6 7 8 9 0   DOC/DOC   1 9 8 7 6 5 4 3

ISBN   978-0-07-182751-5
MHID   0-07-182751-X

e-ISBN 978-0-07-182752-2
e-MHID   0-07-182752-8

Library of Congress Cataloging-in-Publication Data

Crainer, Stuart.
  Thinkers50 leadership : organizational success through leadership / by Stuart Crainer and Des Dearlov.
      pages cm
  Includes index.
  ISBN 978-0-07-182751-5 (alk. paper) — ISBN 0-07-182751-X (alk. paper)
  1. Leadership. 2. Organizational effectiveness. I. Dearlove, Des. II. Title.
  HD57.7.C695   2014
  658.4'092—dc23

                                                                    2013030617

McGraw-Hill Education books are available at special quantity discounts to use as premiums and sales promotions or for use in corporate training programs. To contact a representative, please visit the Contact Us pages at www.mhprofessional.com.

Contents

Introduction

In recent years, we have interviewed a profusion of people from around the world and asked them for their insights concerning leadership—managers in multinationals, a brain surgeon, the board of a Japanese corporation, not-for-profit leaders, a soccer coach, social entrepreneurs, a chef, CEOs, would-be CEOs, MBA students, educational leaders, teachers, and many more.

What is interesting is that virtually all of these people have an opinion on the subject. Often we have been surprised by how nuanced and sophisticated their views are. They have read about the subject and thought about it deeply.

The leadership landscape has shifted. Once leadership was the preserve of the few—military and political figureheads. Now it has been democratized, based on the realization that leadership touches all of our lives each and every day.

As the range of appreciation and the practice of leadership have spread, so, too, has the range of leadership competencies. Leadership is now multifaceted rather than simply being summed up in the dread words *command and control*. Leadership is about feelings. Leadership is about emotions. Leadership is about those who follow. Leadership is about the people who are touched by the actions of leaders.

A while ago, we attended a big soccer match at Wembley Stadium in London. As we were buying the traditional halftime burger, we saw that the burger seller had "Team Leader" proudly emblazoned on his shirt. We got talking as the halftime rush subsided. "We saw the title on your shirt," we said. "What does leadership mean to you?" His response was immediate: "Two words: *by example.*"

This is, perhaps, proof that our understanding of leadership has moved on and that inspiration for those who lead can be found in surprising places. When we talked to Warren Bennis, the leadership thinker who has worked with American presidents and helped shape the field, we asked him what would be the one question he would ask the leaders of the world. "How do you learn?" he replied.

This book combines our experiences talking to practitioners in the field of leadership and the world's leading thinkers on the subject, including Warren Bennis, Jim Collins, Syd Finkelstein, Stew Friedman, Rob Goffee, Marshall Goldsmith, Barbara Kellerman, Rakesh Khurana, Liz Mellon, and many others. Our aim is to give you direct access to, and understanding of, the fundamentals of leadership and the latest thinking on the subject. For leaders, there is a lot to learn.

Stuart Crainer and Des Dearlove
Thinkers50 Founders

CHAPTER

1

How We Got Here

Every year, thousands of books are published on the subject of leadership and leadership development. Reams of papers and masses of Internet pages are devoted to this subject, which has fascinated leaders, would-be leaders, and followers alike for centuries.

Yet despite this great outpouring of leadership-related thinking, we seem to be no closer to discovering the secrets of great leadership. What makes a great leader? Can anyone be a leader, or is it the preserve of a chosen few? Why do people follow one person through hardship and danger, and not another?

These are questions that have been asked throughout the ages. From Julius Caesar to Steve Jobs, we have dissected, discussed, and analyzed what makes great leaders tick. And yet we are still searching for the answers. The magic ingredients for effective leadership remain elusive.

Take even the most basic question: What is leadership? If you survey 100 executives, the chances are that you will get as many different responses. Ask the experts, the academics who spend their lives researching the subject, and you will still be searching for a definitive, broadly accepted answer.

As Tom Peters once put it: "If we're going to make any headway in figuring out the new rules of leadership, we might as well say it up front: There is no one-size-fits-all approach to leadership. Leadership mantra #1: It all depends."

Of course, there are many authoritative opinions and perspectives, some of which are captured in this book. "A leader is a dealer in hope," Napoleon once observed, for example. And he should have known. Or as celebrated leadership guru Warren Bennis noted almost two centuries later, "Managers are people who do things right, and leaders are people who do the right thing."[1]

Does it really matter? Clearly, it does. Imagine a world without leadership. Stop to consider what leadership brings to the world and the effect it has on your daily life at work—and at home.

Take leading an organization, for example. Leading a major organization has never been so challenging, so transient—or, in many cases, so richly rewarded. Nor has the job ever attracted so much critical attention. In recent years, numerous CEOs around the world have fallen from grace, accompanied by some serious soul-searching about the competence and ethical standards of leaders.

Even if there has not been a wholesale crisis of leadership at every level, events over the last decade or so have been serious enough to provoke some rethinking of leadership theory, and to prompt the discussion of a number of new approaches.

In the modern world, with all its interconnectedness, rapid and widespread communication, and globalization of economies and societies, the actions of a single corporate leader can have alarmingly significant ramifications for the well-being of billions of people. They can trigger the collapse of companies, market slumps, global recessions, and rioting on the streets of nations. Or they can herald a period of growth and prosperity, accompanied by the much-sought-after feel-good factor.

The CEOs of some companies are as powerful as kings and presidents, generals and prime ministers. With that kind of power comes tremendous responsibility. And even if they are not the CEO of a huge multinational, sitting astride global commerce, leaders in corporations of all sizes have importance and influence. They may not have the power to bring nations to their knees, but they do have the power to increase the well-being of their followers, to improve the performance of their organizations, to keep their customers satisfied, to make or break individual careers, and to contribute to national prosperity.

Thus the study of leaders and leadership, despite the many disparate theories and ideas, is remarkably important. To know the development of leadership theory is to understand the nature of leadership itself. Theory and practice are inextricably intertwined.

Ancient to Modern

What then has been the evolution of leadership theory and its study? Leadership has fascinated people through the millennia.

Back in the days of the ancient Greeks, the poet Homer wrote about heroes such as Achilles and Odysseus. Likewise, in his book *Parallel Lives*, the Greek historian Plutarch chronicled the histories of great men, including Roman emperors like Julius Caesar. Later, in the Victorian age, Thomas Carlyle dissected the characters of Napoleon and others in his book *On Heroes, Hero-Worship, and the Heroic in History.*

Early leadership theory tended to focus on three broad dimensions of leadership. The first dimension concerned the personality, traits, and attributes of leaders—their general disposition. The second focused on the actions of leaders and the different roles they adopted; it was about what leaders did and how they behaved rather than their characteristics. A third collection of theories clustered around the notion that leadership is specific to its context. Different situations require different styles of leadership.

An early preoccupation of students of leadership was power and influence. Leadership was seen as a function of power, exercised through political and influencing skills. It was a topic that attracted the interest of the Florentine diplomat Niccolò Machiavelli, author of that Renaissance leadership bestseller *The Prince* and an early scholar of human nature in general and leadership in particular.

Machiavelli's ethics were a little dubious. He strongly advocated the use of a combination of cunning and intimidation as a means of effective leadership, underpinned by the idea that the ends justify the means. "Politics have no relation to morals," he said. Many people would argue that this is still the case.

A few centuries later, in the 1950s, social psychologists John French and Bertram Raven examined the relationship between leadership, power, and influence. Where does the power on which leadership is based come from? They identified five sources of the power base for leaders: reward and coercion (the ability of the individual to reward or punish others); referent (the level of popularity that an individual enjoys); legitimate (the power someone derives from his or her position within an organization); and expert (power based on an individual's specialized knowledge and competence).[2]

Nature or Nurture

Possibly the most common question asked about leadership is whether leaders are born or made. Is it nature or nurture that leaders have to thank for their position? A long-held view was that leaders were born with innate talents that could not be taught. This was the Great Man theory, which was popular in the nineteenth and early twentieth centuries. (Not Great Woman theory, however, as their successes as leaders were generally disregarded at that time—and depressingly often thereafter.)

Closely associated with the notion of great men, colossi of the leadership world, was Trait theory. This discipline seeks to identify universal leadership characteristics or traits. It suggests that great leaders have certain personality traits, characteristics, and attributes in common that mark them as leaders. Therefore, in theory, it should be possible to study large numbers of leaders and identify those common traits.

That is exactly what Warren Bennis set out to do in the mid-1980s with his famous study of American leaders (see Chapter 2). Bennis wanted to codify effective leadership. In place of the man or woman of destiny, he offered a view of leadership based on a platform of discrete characteristics.

Great Man (and Woman) theory and Trait theory have fallen out of favor over the years. Yet despite the many critics of these theories, leadership researchers are frequently enticed by the prospect of surveying collections of leaders, identifying common characteristics among them, and extrapolating those characteristics to leadership in general.

In the 1960s, and over the following decade or two, attention shifted to the way the leader led—the leader's actions and behavior. For example, management theorists Robert Blake and Jane Mouton developed the managerial grid model, which classified managers according to styles, with particular focus on the dimensions of tasks and people.[3] There are five main managerial styles. They range from a 1/1, a do-nothing manager who does very little and has no regard for people or tasks, through to a 9/9 leader, who combines great people motivation with consummate organizational skills.

In the 1970s and 1980s, the British thinker John Adair shifted the focus to key leadership functions (planning, initiating, controlling, supporting, informing, and evaluating) and areas of leadership responsibility (task, team, and individual). His Action Centered Leadership (ACL) concept was a more practical approach to leadership evaluation, with the leader's job being to focus on task achievement, team building, and motivating team members.[4]

There were other perspectives on the leadership styles or functions, too. Leaders were divided into those who were *directive* and those who were *participative*, for example. Directive leaders gave orders and instructions, taking decisions on behalf of their teams and expecting their subordinates to follow. In contrast, participative leaders attempted to get buy-in from their followers through a more consultative decision-making process.

Context Is King

Leadership researchers also explored the role of the situation or context in leadership. Some leaders are effective during one period and then not during another. Winston Churchill was an effective leader in wartime, but not in peacetime, for example. Perhaps different situations and contexts require different leadership styles.

This is the essence of *situational theory*. From this comes *contingency theory*, in which situational variables are taken into account to select the most appropriate leadership style in a given set of circumstances.

Situational leadership is closely associated with Paul Hersey, a former professor of leadership and author of *The Situational Leader*, and Ken Blanchard, of *The One Minute Manager* fame, who is currently chief spiritual officer of the Ken Blanchard Companies. The two initially developed their model while collaborating on the first edition of *The Management of Organizational Behavior* in 1969. Initially called the life-cycle theory of leadership, by 1977 it had been revised to the slightly less catchy situational leadership theory.[5]

Blanchard and Hersey identified four leadership styles that could be used in different situations: *telling*, an autocratic style for when subordinates appeared unable or unwilling to do what is required; *selling*, which is sometimes seen as a coaching-type style; *participating*, where there is shared decision making between the leader and the followers, and the leader adopts a facilitating role; and *delegating*, which, once the leader has identified the task, involves handing responsibility for carrying it out to the followers.

Meanwhile, psychologist Fred E. Fiedler outlined a contingency leadership model in which effectiveness is related to two factors: *leadership style* and *situational control*—the control and influence conferred on the leader because of the situation. These depended on a number of other factors, such as the relationship between the leader and his or her followers, whether the task is a structured task or not, and how much power the leader has within the organization.[6]

Leadership, Relatively Speaking

Perhaps the biggest shake-up in the leadership field happened with the work of political scientist James MacGregor Burns in the late 1970s. Burns introduced the idea that there were two contrasting leadership styles: *transactional* and *transformational* leadership. In the first, there is a mutually beneficial relationship between the leader and the follower that meets the needs of both parties. In contrast, transformational leadership is about the two parties engaging, understanding each other's motivations, and entering into a binding and mutually stimulating relationship. Transformational leaders take the leader-follower interaction to a different level.[7]

Transformational leadership has been one of the dominant concepts in leadership theory since the 1970s. In turn, the transformational leadership baton has been picked up by numerous academics who have developed different facets of the concept.

The first was Bernard Bass, who introduced four components of transformational leadership. *Idealized influence* stems from the moral and ethical standards of the leader: the leader acts as a role model who is admired and respected by the followers; *inspirational motivation* spurs followers to undertake shared goals; *intellectual stimulation* encourages independent thinking, argument, discourse, rational thinking, and problem solving; and *individualized consideration* occurs when the leader gives the followers personal attention and advice.[8]

The concept attracted widespread interest. Not surprisingly, the idea of an inspirational leader, who engages the emotions of individuals, is more appealing than that of a transactional leader, who is interested only in the "If I do this for you, then you do this in return" aspect of the relationship, and will use rewards and punishment to get his or her way.

Leaders Drive Change

Leadership theory has been revisited more recently in the context of change. MIT's Edgar Schein, and later Harvard Business School's John Kotter and Rosabeth Moss Kanter, have tackled change leadership, for example.

Kanter has looked at the leaders who excel at dealing with change—the change masters—and has also researched turnaround leadership in detail. Based on studies of several turnarounds, she suggests that information and relationships are crucial elements. A turnaround leader must facilitate a psychological change of attitudes and behavior before organizational recovery can take place. She identifies four essential components of the turnaround process: promoting dialogue, engendering respect, sparking collaboration, and inspiring initiative.

A related concept is the idea of tipping point leadership. The notion of the tipping point was popularized in Malcolm Gladwell's book with that title.[9] Gladwell looked at how the emergence of a fashion trend is similar to the spread of infections and the science of epidemiology. This is not an orderly process. "Ideas and products and messages and behaviors spread just like viruses do," with just a few carriers being necessary to spread a cultural infection. The progress of the new idea soon comes to follow a rapid upward curve, hitting critical mass at the "tipping point."

Effective and innovative ideas in leadership can progress in a similar way. W. Chan Kim and Renée Mauborgne, professors at the international business school INSEAD, produced a compelling riff on this concept in their idea of "tipping point leadership," exemplified by former New York police chief William Bratton (see Chapter 8).[10]

Reinventing Leadership

Elsewhere, psychologist and former New York Times journalist Daniel Goleman has argued that leaders need to be emotionally intelligent (EI). IQ alone is not enough. Managers need to understand and manage their own emotions and relationships if they are to be effective leaders. Goleman's ideas on emotional intelligence build on the work of David McClelland, a U.S. psychological theorist who helped establish competencies modeling and was Goleman's mentor at Harvard, and Howard Gardner, a developmental psychologist and professor of cognition and education at the Harvard Graduate School of Education at Harvard University, who developed the theory of multiple intelligences.

In *Primal Leadership*, Goleman advocates cultivating emotionally intelligent leaders.[11] Goleman and his coauthors, Richard E. Boyatzis and Annie McKee, explain the four domains of emotional intelligence—self-awareness, self-management, social awareness, and relationship management—and how they give rise to different styles of leadership. It is a leadership repertoire that leaders can master and use to great effect.

Finally, some academics are adopting a more radical take on leadership for the twenty-first century.

Some argue that leadership is distributed across teams. Wharton's Katherine J. Klein spent 10 months studying medical teams in action at the Baltimore Shock Trauma Center. Her close-up view of leadership in action led her to adopt a unique perspective on leadership "as a system or a structure—a characteristic not of individuals but of the organization or unit as a whole."

In the fraught, pressured conditions in which the trauma unit worked, where poor decisions or wasted seconds might mean the difference between life and death, leadership was "a role—or, more specifically, a dynamic, socially enabled and socially constrained set of functions which may be filled by the numerous individuals who, over time, occupy key positions of expert authority on the team."[12]

In such a situation, leadership was the product of the organization or unit's "norms, routines and role definitions." The function of the leader existed separately from the many different people who filled the role depending on the circumstances.

Klein identified four key leadership functions: providing strategic direction, monitoring team performance, instructing team members, and providing hands-on assistance when required.

Based on Klein's findings, organizations should put in place the structures needed to support whoever steps into a leadership position—have well-established roles and clearly identified norms—rather than concentrate on selecting brilliant leaders.

Others, such as Lynda Gratton, a professor at London Business School, argue that leadership is a role that helps employees fulfill their aspirations in an organizational democracy in which they are the citizens rather than mere employees. Gratton describes such a scenario in her book *The Democratic Enterprise*.[13]

Leadership Avenues

And yet, despite all the millions of words devoted to the subject of leadership, we are still waiting for a definitive, universally accepted definition of leadership. If anything, ideas about leadership have become more fragmented.

Traditional concepts associated with leadership, such as traits and style, are still considered important, and heroic celebrity CEOs are still very much in evidence in some organizations. At the same time, new approaches, such as quiet leadership, authentic leadership, followership, and distributed leadership, have come to the fore.

But what can be said is that when it comes to understanding leadership, we have moved from directive leadership and leadership derived from authority and power to a greater belief in the interactive nature of leadership and leadership by consent.

And while leadership used to focus on CEOs and senior executives, generals and presidents, and kings and queens, it is no longer fixated solely on the apex of the organizational hierarchy. It is generally accepted that leaders exist throughout organizations, and that they all require as much support and attention as the leaders at the top.

What we can say with some certainty, however, is that new ideas about leadership continue to emerge. Many centuries after people first began exploring the fundamentals of leadership, the field of leadership is still evolving.

In the chapters that follow, we pick out some common threads among the tangled web of modern leadership theory.

Chapter 2: Crucibles of Leadership

Leadership, says Warren Bennis, is founded on deeply felt experiences. Although youth is not necessarily a barrier to being a leader, young leaders should preferably have been through a crucible and emerged unscathed on the other side.

By a crucible, Bennis told us, he means "utterly transforming events or tests that individuals must pass through and make meaning from in order to learn, grow, and lead."

The challenge for youthful leaders is that crucibles are rare and cannot be artificially reproduced. For many older leaders, World War II and the Great Depression of the 1930s were crucibles in which their values were formed. The next generation of leaders will have to find other experiences to forge their leadership talent and commitment.

Chapter 3: Level 5 Leadership

Leaders not only need to be in touch with their own and others' emotions, but also need to be humble, according to Jim Collins, the author of the 2001 bestseller *Good to Great* (and coauthor of the 1994 bestseller *Built to Last*).[14] Collins champions Level 5 Leadership, a combination of selflessness, humility, and iron will. These leaders are usually "quiet leaders," not the larger-than-life charismatic heroes who are much feted by Wall Street and the City. For leadership, humility is the final frontier.

Chapter 4: The Real Thing

If heroic leadership is "out," authentic leadership is definitely "in." Authentic leadership is the antidote to the leadership excesses of the star leaders. We can't all be heroes, but we can all be true to ourselves. Leadership is within everyone's reach.

In part, authentic leadership reflects the backlash against heroic leadership and trait theory. Proponents of the concept include Bill George, the former CEO of Medtronic, and business school academics such as Rob Goffee and Gareth Jones.

With authentic leadership, the best leaders make the most of the qualities that they already possess. They trade on their strengths and understand their weaknesses. To be useful, these qualities must be real, perceived by others, and significant. Authentic leadership is definitely not about adopting the styles or traits of other successful leaders.

Authentic leadership requires introspection and heightened self-awareness. Leaders who take shortcuts, skipping these necessary stages of self-development, could adopt false personas that are not true to their own values or beliefs.

Leaders who take on fake personas can be highly damaging to organizations, especially if they are using their fake personas and their leadership to compensate for perceived personal short-comings.

Chapter 5: Charisma and the Dark Side

One avenue of exploration has been the merits of heroic and charismatic leadership, and the darker side of leadership. In the late 1990s, Michael Maccoby noted a pronounced change in the personality of those at the top of companies. The new breed of business leaders craved the limelight. "There's something new and daring about the CEOs who are transforming today's industries," he observed.[15] In Maccoby's view, these larger-than-life leaders closely resembled the personality type that Sigmund Freud described as narcissistic. And while narcissistic leadership was not necessarily a bad thing, it might easily be.

Charismatic leadership is linked to narcissistic leadership, and this is an idea developed by the sociologist Max Weber and several leadership theorists, including Jay Conger of Claremont McKenna College.

Charismatic leaders figure prominently throughout history, including such figures as Napoleon, Churchill, and Gandhi. But while charisma was once considered a desirable, even necessary leadership quality, its benefits as an attribute are increasingly being questioned.

Chapter 6: Followership

One effect of transformational theory was to focus attention on the leader-follower relationship. "Managing Your Boss," a

1980 article by two Harvard professors, John Kotter and John Gabarro, cast the manager-boss relationship as one of mutual dependence.[16] And, they argued, if the relationship was not especially good, the follower should take the time to cultivate a more productive working relationship.

A few years later, in 1988, "In Praise of Followers" by Robert Kelley, a consultant and an academic, appeared in the *Harvard Business Review*, placing the idea of followership at center stage.[17]

In *Followership*, Barbara Kellerman of Harvard University's John F. Kennedy School of Government asks where leaders would be without good followers. It is a particularly relevant question in an age when, says Kellerman, "Cultural constraints against taking on people in positions of power, authority, and influence have been weakened." As she also notes, "Followers are gaining power and influence while leaders are losing power and influence."[18]

Chapter 7: Where Leaders Meet the World

Leadership does not exist in a corporate and organizational vacuum. It affects and overlaps with the rest of your life. But how can work and life be balanced, and what does this mean for leadership?

Chapter 8: Leaders at Work

There is nothing so practical as a great theory. But where does this leave leadership, a hugely practical discipline bedeviled by a profusion of bright ideas and often fuzzily defined concepts?

CHAPTER

2

Crucibles of Leadership

There is a moment in the life of a leader when the leader makes the grade, when he or she leaps from management to leadership, from team member to leader. For Warren Bennis, that moment came when he was the youngest infantry officer in the European theater of operations during World War II. This experience was what Bennis later called a *crucible*.

"A crucible is by definition a transformative experience though which an individual comes to a new or an altered sense of identity," Bennis wrote.[1]

The crucible experience was instrumental in shaping the leadership qualities of the people that Bennis later interviewed. "We found that something magical happens in the crucible—an alchemy whereby fear and suffering are transformed into something glorious and redemptive. This process reveals, if it does not create, leadership, the ability to inspire and move others to action."[2]

These people were able to take the event, whether it was fighting in a war, some disaster, or another significant event in their life, good or bad, and construct a narrative around it—about the challenge, how they dealt with it, learned from it, and became better leaders as a result.

On Fire

Bennis is white-toothed, permanently tanned, and California-based. He *looks* like a leader. We have talked with him numerous times over the last 20 or so years. He is an enthusiastic interviewee and person. Discussing the concept of crucibles, we asked him about creating a crucible.

> *Is it possible for people to create their own crucible?*
> That's the big question. I think crucibles are created all the time. We all experience crucibles, but what do we do at the back end of them? Do we learn from them? Do we extract wisdom from them? I have been puzzling about how we create within our institutions the capacity to understand what goes on when organizations or individuals face crucibles. It isn't a question of how we create them; they happen almost all the time. Do we think of them as a dream, so that when we wake up and brush our teeth, they vaporize, or do we think about the dream and learn from it?

It is the same thing with the crucibles: having to fire people, being fired, being shipped to an office you don't like, or thinking that you have been demoted when maybe you haven't been. It's a matter of how an organization can use the crucibles of everyday life and extract wisdom from them to make the organization learn organically from the experiences it's undergoing. My concern is, how do we use everyday crucibles that we're sometimes not conscious of.

So leaders have to seek out uncertainty?
You can't create Mandela's Robben Island or John McCain's experiences in Vietnam. They are extreme.

You can't be held responsible for the era in which you live.
President Clinton was always slightly envious of other presidents because he didn't have a war to deal with that would let him prove himself. Teddy Roosevelt was the same, although he had a few minor skirmishes.

There is a view that the leaders who are around now were shaped by the 1960s, which was a fractious time in the United States. They didn't experience a crucible like World War II or the Depression.

You could look at this generation of geeks and say that their formative period ended at 9/11, but it started in 1989 when the Berlin Wall fell and the Cold War ended, and then there was the introduction of the World Wide Web. So it's not a generational thing; it affects a shorter period.

*If we are creatures of circumstance, doesn't that mean
we are powerless?*

That's right. One of our grand old men of leadership,
John Gardner, had been a marine in World War II
and worked with President Johnson. He was shy
and introverted, but he was plunged into leadership.
I interviewed him during a week when I also interviewed a couple of young guys who had had to lay
off 25 of their friends from their business. I asked
Gardner what he thought would create more angst,
more emotional charge: being in the war or firing
some of your closest friends. He was unsure.

But events on a cosmic scale, when you're thinking about what might happen to the world, are profoundly different from being sent to work in another
country for your employer.

*Your experiences in the war were obviously a cruci-
ble for you, but did you emerge from that thinking of
yourself as a leader?*

I do think of myself now as a thought leader. I came
from a very poor family, so after the war, I was thinking that I'd got through it and felt okay about what I
had done as a young officer, and then I was stationed
in Frankfurt after the war, and I had a Jeep and an
apartment, and it was quite a good life. What I had
learned was discipline and a sense of self-mastery. I
felt that I took care of myself and was motivated to
learn more. I thought, now I am ready to face life, but
I didn't feel as though I was a leader. I stayed on until

April 1947. It shaped me so much and pulled from me things I might not otherwise have experienced. I was very shy, and I felt that I was a boring human being, and then in the course of being in the army, I felt that I was more interesting to myself. It was a coming of age.[3]

After the Fire

After the war, Bennis was an undergraduate at Antioch College, studying under Douglas McGregor, creator of the motivational concept of Theory X and Theory Y. Later, Bennis followed McGregor to Massachusetts Institute of Technology (MIT), where he received his PhD in economics and social science. He went on to join the school's faculty and was chairman of the Organization Studies Department. "My early work was on small group dynamics, more a classical area of social psychology. I moved from there to T-groups, sensitivity training, and then change in social systems," recalls Bennis.

After being an early student of group dynamics in the 1950s, Bennis became a futurologist in the 1960s. His work—particularly *The Temporary Society* (1968)—explored new organizational forms.[4] For Bennis, organizations needed to become *adhocracies*—roughly the opposite of bureaucracies—freed from the shackles of hierarchy and meaningless paperwork. (The term *adhocracies* was later used by Alvin Toffler, among others.)

At the same time that he was predicting potential futures for the business world, Bennis was confronting the sometimes frustrating realties of being a leader: as a university administrator, provost, and executive vice president at the State University of New York at Buffalo, and as president of the University of Cincinnati. While the field of leadership theory was where his passion lay, the practice did not live up to his expectations.

"When I was at the University of Cincinnati, I realized that I was seeking power through position, by being president of the university. I wanted to *be* a university president, but I didn't want to *do* it. I wanted the influence," he says. "In the end, I wasn't very good at being a president. I looked out the window and thought that the man who was cutting the lawn actually seemed to have more control over what he was doing."

Bennis returned to what he enjoyed most: teaching, researching, consulting, writing, and speaking about leadership. Today he is a distinguished professor of business administration and professor of management and organization at the University of Southern California (USC) Marshall School of Business in Los Angeles, where he founded the school's Leadership Institute. He also chairs the advisory board of the Center for Public Leadership at Harvard University's Kennedy School of Government.

"I have been thinking about leadership almost as long as I have been thinking," he says. "It is probably a trap of my own making. My first major article came out in 1959 and was on leadership. Since 1985 most of my work has been in that area. You build up some sort of brand equity and there is a degree of collusion between that and the marketplace—people say leadership that's Bennis. It makes life a little simpler."[5]

On Leaders

In 1985, *Leaders: The Strategies for Taking Charge* was published, coauthored by Bennis and Burt Nanus, founder and director of the Center of Futures Research at the University of Southern California.[6] The book is based on research examining the lives of 90 of America's best-known leaders. The eclectic mix of names included McDonald's founder Ray Kroc; many other people from the worlds of business, sports, and the arts; and even an astronaut, Neil Armstrong

"They were right-brained and left-brained, tall and short, fat and thin, articulate and inarticulate, assertive and retiring, dressed for success and dressed for failure, participative and autocratic," says Bennis.[7] But despite their diversity, they were united in one thing at least: they had all shown "mastery over present confusion."

From these leaders, Bennis and Nanus identified four common abilities: management of attention, meaning, trust, and self. Managing meaning involves the effective use of communications skills and technology to bring the vision to life and make it real. Effective communication is about analogy, metaphor, vivid illustration, emotion, trust, optimism, and hope.

Trust is the "the emotional glue that binds followers and leaders together." Among other things, trust is underpinned by consistency. The final thing that the leaders that Bennis studied shared was "deployment of self." Becoming a good leader requires hard work. The emphasis is on persistence and self-knowledge, taking risks, commitment, and challenge, but, above all, on learning. "The learning person looks forward to failure or mistakes," says Bennis. "The worst problem in leadership is basically early success. There's no opportunity to learn from adversity and problems."[8]

The leaders also possess "emotional wisdom," a positive self-regard. This wisdom is characterized by an ability to accept people as they are; a capacity to approach things in terms of only the present; an ability to treat everyone with courteous attention; an ability to trust others, even when this seems to be a risky strategy; and the capacity to go without constant approval and recognition.

Learning to Lead

As Bennis powerfully and repeatedly suggests, leadership can be learned, and this lies at the heart of his work, and of *Leaders* in particular: "Every person has to make a genuine contribution in their lives. The institution of work is one of the main vehicles to achieving this. I'm more and more convinced that individual leaders can create a human community that will, in the long run, lead to the best organizations."[9]

However, to achieve this, we need to overcome five myths about leadership. First, leadership is not a rare skill. Second, leaders are made rather than born. Third, leaders are mostly ordinary, or apparently ordinary, people, rather than being charismatic. Fourth, leadership is not limited to the people at the top of the organization; it is relevant at all levels. Finally, leadership is not about control, direction, and manipulation; it is about aligning people's energy with an attractive goal.

Later, in *On Becoming a Leader*, Bennis turned his attention to a common question in organizations: What is the difference between managers and leaders? It is an important distinction, says Bennis.

"To survive in the twenty-first century we're going to need a new generation of leaders, not managers. The distinction is an important one. Leaders conquer the context—the volatile, turbulent, ambiguous surroundings that sometimes seek to conspire against us and will surely suffocate us if we let them—while managers surrender to it."[10]

Bennis helpfully provides a list of fundamental differences between managers and leaders:

- The manager administers; the leader innovates.
- The manager is a copy; the leader is an original.
- The manager maintains; the leader develops.
- The manager focuses on systems and structure; the leader focuses on people.
- The manager relies on control; the leader inspires trust.
- The manager has a short-range view; the leader has a long-range perspective.
- The manager asks how and when; the leader asks what and why.
- The manager has his eye on the bottom line; the leader has his eye on the horizon.
- The manager accepts the status quo; the leader challenges it.
- The manager is the classic good soldier; the leader is his own person.
- The manager does things right; the leader does the right thing.[11]

Leading with Others

By the mid-1990s, Bennis was exploring group working and cooperative leadership. In his 1997 book, *Organizing Genius*, Bennis turned his attention to the power of groups, how groups organize, and the role of leadership in groups.

He describes the work and achievements of outstanding groups such as Lockheed's Skunk Works; the research team involved in the Manhattan Project, which invented the atomic bomb; and Xerox's legendary Palo Alto Research Center.

Leaders are an essential element of a great group, although it is not the leader that makes the group great, but rather all the people in the group and their interaction.

Once again Bennis questions the notion of the heroic leader. The heroic view of the leader as the indomitable individual is now outdated and inappropriate. "He or she is a pragmatic dreamer, a person with an original but attainable vision. Ironically, the leader is able to realize his or her dream only if the others are free to do exceptional work."[12]

Rather than impose themselves on the group, leaders have to find a way to lead that fits in with the group. "Inevitably, the leader has to invent a leadership style that suits the group. The standard models, especially command and control, simply don't work. The heads of groups have to act decisively, but never arbitrarily. They have to make decisions without limiting the perceived autonomy of the other participants. Devising and maintaining an atmosphere in which others can put a dent in the universe is the leader's creative act."[13]

About the same time as *Organizing Genius* was published, Bennis was also researching the teams of leaders below the CEO, who are often the people getting things done in the organization. So in *Co-Leaders: The Power of Great Partnerships* (1996), Bennis and his coauthor, David A. Heenan, a visiting professor at Georgetown University, looked past Bill Gates, who was CEO of Microsoft at the time, to look at his deputy, Steve Ballmer.[14] They also examined many other coleaders to understand the relationships between the leader and the led and to discern commonalities.

By the 2000s, Bennis was championing what he called the "new leadership." He argued that fragmentation of the value chain required leadership of a different kind, where the ability to influence was a highly prized skill.

We talked to Bennis about new leadership and his work on groups.

Do you see yourself as a romantic?
If a romantic is someone who believes in possibilities and who is optimistic, then that is probably an accurate description. I think that every person has to make a genuine contribution in life, and the institution of work is one of the main vehicles for achieving this. I'm more and more convinced that individual leaders can create a human community that will, in the long run, lead to the best organizations.

Do great groups require great leaders?
Greatness starts with superb people. Great groups don't exist without great leaders, but they give the lie to the persistent notion that successful institutions are the lengthened shadow of a great woman or man. It's not clear that life was ever so simple that individuals, acting alone, could solve most significant problems. None of us is as smart as all of us.

So, the John Wayne type of hero is a thing of the past?
Yes, the Lone Ranger is dead. Instead of the individual problem solver, we have a new model for creative

achievement. People like Steve Jobs and Walt Disney headed groups and found their own greatness in them. The new leader is a pragmatic dreamer, a person with an original but attainable vision. Ironically, the leader is able to realize his or her dream only if the others are free to do exceptional work. Typically, the leader is the one who recruits the others, by making the vision so palpable and seductive that they see it, too, and eagerly sign up.

But isn't this somewhat unrealistic?

True. Most organizations are dull, and working life is mundane. There is no getting away from that. So, these groups could be an inspiration. A great group is more than a collection of first-rate minds. It's a miracle. I have unwarranted optimism. By looking at the possibilities, we can all improve.

What will it take for future leaders to be effective?

The postbureaucratic organization requires a new kind of alliance between the leaders and the led. Today's organizations are evolving into federations, networks, clusters, cross-functional teams, temporary systems, ad hoc task forces, lattices, modules, matrices—almost anything but pyramids with their obsolete top-down leadership. The new leader will encourage healthy dissent and values those followers who are courageous enough to say no.

This does not mark the end of leadership—rather, it indicates the need for a new, far more subtle and indirect form of influence if leaders are to be effective. The new reality is that intellectual capital (brainpower, know-how, and human imagination) has supplanted capital as the critical success factor, and leaders will have to learn an entirely new set of skills that are not understood, are not taught in our business schools, and, for all of those reasons, are rarely practiced. Four competencies will determine the success of new leadership.

What's the first?

The new leader understands and practices the power of appreciation. These leaders are connoisseurs of talent, more curators than creators. The leader is rarely the best or the brightest in the new organizations. New leaders have a smell for talent, an imaginative Rolodex, and are unafraid of hiring people who are better than they are. In my research into great groups, I found that in most cases, the leader was rarely the cleverest or the sharpest. Peter Schneider, president of Disney's colossally successful Feature Animation studio, leads a group of 1,200 animators. He can't draw to save his life. Bob Taylor, former head of the Palo Alto Research Center, where the first commercial PC was invented, wasn't a computer scientist. Max De Pree put it best when he said that good leaders "abandon their ego to the talents of others."

Then, what's next?

The new leader keeps reminding people of what's important. Organizations drift into entropy and the bureaucratization of imagination when they forget what's important. It's simple to say, but that one sentence is one of the few pieces of advice I suggest to leaders: remind your people of what's important. A powerful enough vision can transform what would otherwise be routine and drudgery into collectively focused energy. Witness the Manhattan Project. The U.S. Army had recruited talented engineers from all over the United States for special duty on the project. They were assigned to work on the primitive computers of the period (1943–1945), doing energy calculations and other tedious jobs.

But the army was obsessed with security and refused to tell them anything specific about the project. They didn't know that they were building a weapon that could end the war or even what their calculations meant. They were simply expected to do the work, which they did slowly and not very well. Richard Feynman, who supervised the technicians, prevailed on his superiors to tell the recruits what they were doing and why. Permission to lift the veil of secrecy was granted, and Robert Oppenheimer gave them a special lecture on the nature of the project and their own contribution.

"Complete transformation," Feynman recalled. "They began to invent ways of doing it better. They improved the scheme. They worked at night. They didn't need supervising in the night; they didn't need anything. They understood everything; they invented several of the programs we used." Feynman calculated that the work was done "nearly 10 times as fast" after it had meaning.

Charles Handy has it right in his book *The Hungry Spirit*. We are all hungry spirits craving purpose and meaning at work, to contribute something beyond ourselves, and leaders must never forget to remind people of what's important.

What else does a new leader strive for?

The new leader generates and sustains trust. We're all aware that the terms of the new social contract of work have changed. No one can depend on lifelong loyalty or commitment to any organization. Since 1985, about 25 percent of the American workforce has been laid off at least once. At a time when the new social contract makes the ties between organizations and their knowledge workers tenuous, trust becomes the emotional glue that can bond people to an organization.

Trust is a small word with powerful connotations and is a hugely complex factor. The ingredients are a combination of competencies, constancy, caring, fairness, candor, and authenticity—most of all, the last. And the new leaders achieve that when they can successfully balance the tripod of forces that are working on and in most of us: ambition, competence, and integrity.

And the last competency?

The new leader and the led are intimate allies. The power of Steven Spielberg's *Schindler's List* lies in the transformation of Schindler from a sleazy, down-at-the-heels, small-time con man who moves to Poland in order to harness cheap Jewish labor to make munitions that he can then sell to the Germans at low cost. His transformation comes over a period of time during which he interacts with his Jewish workers, most of all the accountant, Levin, but there are also frequent and achingly painful moments where he confronts the evil of the war and of the Holocaust. In the penultimate scene, when the war is over and the Nazis have evacuated the factory, but before the American troops arrive, the prisoners give him a ring that they have made for him from the precious metals that the workers used. As he tries to put the ring on, he begins crying, "Why, why are you doing this? With this metal, we could have saved three, maybe four, maybe five more Jews." And he drives off in tears.

It is hard to be objective about this scene, but, although this was a unique, singular event, it portrays what the new leadership is all about: that great leaders are made by great groups and by organizations that create the social architecture of respect and dignity. These new leaders will not have the loudest voices, but they will have the most attentive ears. Instead of pyramids, these postbureaucratic organizations will be structures built of energy and ideas, led by people who find their joy in the task at hand, while embracing one another—and not worrying about leaving monuments behind.

If you go into a company, what's the most important question you ask?

On a scale from 1 to 10, with 10 meaning 100 percent and 1 meaning close to zero, how much of your talents are being deployed in your job? And why?

The Heat Is On

For their 2003 book, *Geeks and Geezers: How Era, Values, and Defining Moments Shape Leaders*, Robert Thomas and Bennis interviewed almost 50 leaders: "geeks" (leaders between the ages of 21 and 35) and "geezers" (men and women between the ages of 70 and 93).[15] Despite the differences in age, the two groups of leaders had some important things in common.

The research led to a model of leadership development. Successful leaders had four essential competencies: the ability to engage others through shared meaning, a distinctive and compelling voice, integrity, and adaptive capacity. Of these, adaptive capacity was the most important.

Talking with Bob Thomas, he laid out the genesis of the book:

> I had a student who called me up and told me that he had a very attractive offer to go to work for an Internet start-up and didn't quite know what to do about it. He was currently in a position that was very good. It was a Fortune 50 company, and he was being mentored by the CEO. He had enormous opportunities and possibilities in front of him, and yet he felt

that in some respects, he was going to be living out someone else's script.

And I pressed him about that issue, why writing his own script was so important to him, and his response was, "Well, I've come to recognize that I learn things when I put myself in danger, and it's that kind of experience that I want to reproduce."

I said, "Give me an example of a time when you learned something." He told a story of a time when he was responsible for a plastics plant and someone had done something that was a shortcut. He had created a very unsafe condition; a pipe blew up, and the person was scalded horribly and ultimately died from his injuries.

But my student said that he learned that being a leader is not just about accomplishing the objectives that are set out for you or coming up with creative ways in which to do old things, but somehow it's being a leader of a community. And he had never thought that a business would be a community or that he would ever care that much about the people he was leading because he'd learned through college and elsewhere to be really good with the numbers.

It took that experience to jar him, but the point wasn't simply that he now had to be responsible as a leader of a community. That's an important lesson to learn, but he also learned something else, which is that those kinds of big events, where your back is against the wall or you're encountering something that you've never seen before, are times in which you learn your most important lessons.

He said, "I'm not a thrill seeker. I don't put myself unnecessarily in danger, but I do know that I will learn big things only in those kinds of circumstances."

Going back to the conundrum he had about whether to take a job at a start-up, he said it felt like another one of those opportunities, almost as if the hair on the back of his neck was standing up, telling him that this was an opportunity to learn important things.

I drew from this young man's experience the idea that there are times and places in which one learns much more important things than one does in others. If you get good at spotting them, seeing them approaching, or recognizing that you're in them, you may, in fact, learn valuable new things.

So when Bennis and I did the book, not only did we emphasize the importance of the notion of crucibles and people learning from those kinds of experiences, but there was something else implicit in it, which was to distinguish between the types of lessons that people learned.

There were the lessons that they learned about leadership and about themselves as leaders. Those are important, but when people described them, they were often pretty mundane, the sort of thing that any textbook would capture. It was the second type of lesson that really intrigued me, which is the lessons that they learned about how they learn. If you gain some insight into what it takes for you to learn important things—not just what it takes for you to accumulate knowledge or what it takes for you to become versed in something, but what it takes for you to gain new insight into both who you are and what you could be—then that has to be an accelerant to learning.

Geezer Speak

For the perennially enquiring Bennis, connecting with the younger generation was clearly an opportunity to learn. But we also asked him about the geezers.

Aren't the geezers inevitably more interesting than the geeks?
I would hate to say that, as I am one of them. I would hate to sound biased or judgmental, but they have lived longer and gone through an awful lot. I think what the geeks haven't experienced are the crucibles like World War II and the Depression. During their formative years, they have seen almost uninterrupted prosperity, growth, and success. They are often children of affluence.

September 11 was the first collective shock to the worldview they grew up with. It was a jolt to them.

You talk of the geeks being smothered in possibilities.
Yes. I think it does create anxiety. The world's their oyster, and they can choose what they do. They have so many options and possibilities.

Every year, I teach a class on the art and adventure of leadership to a class of 20-year-olds. They are our best and brightest, but they are so confused that they end up going to law school. I think a third of those who take this class go on to law school because they don't know what else to do. The Asian students are highly vocationally oriented because they are first-generation Americans. They tend to go into science or medicine. They absorb uncertainty through the professions. You see that also with other groups—think of the Jewish expression "my son, the doctor."

But both the geeks and the geezers appear to be very certain of their view of the world?
The work-life balance issue is a real split between the generations. I asked one of the geeks what he would be doing if there wasn't such a thing as a computer. He paused for a long time, then said, "I don't know," and added that he would have been a miserable accountant.

What about the people in between geeks and geezers? Isn't it a kind of no man's land?
When I think about the readership of the book, I think it is probably exactly that group in the middle. Those people should be the buyers. The geeks don't read, and the geezers don't buy books in the business category (although I don't think of this as a business book).

My coauthor kept saying, "What about me?"
That group is not just the one that will buy this book,
but it is an articulating point. These people have the
responsibility, I think, to be the translators, the people who will help each group.

I was talking to my son-in-law, who is 40, and a
lot of his friends who are just a little older are struggling with the Internet and the technology. So it is the
people who are in the middle group, who are comfortable with the technology but are a little wiser and
older, who have to be the articulating point.

*Do you detect that same level of self-awareness in the
geeks you talked to?*
I think that what comes through is that they feel that
they have more license to talk about themselves and
their inner feelings. This is unlike some of the geezers,
who would never dream about talking about their
relations with their family and things like that. There
is a real restraint among the geezers, a kind of reserve,
while those in the younger generation are more free
with their feelings, aspirations, and things like that.

*What about the way we develop leaders? A lot of
people go into MBA programs without a bedrock of
self-awareness.*
Some universities in the United States have two weeks
of induction that concentrates on teamwork, and they
do Myers-Briggs so that the students become quite
aware of who they are. You've got to realize that most

business school faculty members have not actually run anything. They have not done the heavy lifting of actually leading.

I am glad that business schools are now taking people who have worked for three to five years. In many instances, these students have more experience than the faculty.

I am totally in favor of a national service system. It is badly needed. The youth are all dressed up, but they have no place to go. This would not be specifically military service (although I wouldn't exclude the military), but a way for them to get experience before going to law school or business school.

There is a required course on ethics at Harvard Business School, but not at most business schools. It's a very difficult topic, but we need to think about the purpose of education. We have to ask the questions at business schools, "Is there something more important than money? Do corporations exist for something more than money and the bottom line?" Of course they do, but we have to explain it better.

Was there a difference between the geeks and the geezers in terms of their attitudes toward money?
The geezers were brought up in Maslow's survival mode. Often they grew up in some poverty with limited financial aspirations. They thought that earning $10,000 a year would have been enough. Compare that to the geeks, some of whom made a lot of money when they were young. They are operating in a differ-

ent context. If they were broke, they would be more concerned with making a living than with making history.

How can you bridge the gap between the geeks and the geezers?

We must. It would be interesting to hear families discussing the book. I think the geezers may have a more difficult time with the changes that are under way, such as technology. You start to think about your mortality when you are in your sixties, and there is a certain envy of youth. When you are in your sixties, you are no longer promising.

Dialogue between generations is important. A number of companies, including GE, have reverse mentoring, where young people mentor older people to acquaint them with the e-world. There is a lot of ageism, which I probably wouldn't be sensitive to except for the fact I am in my eighties. When people see me in a car, they see white hair, and they behave differently. These will be profound issues for society in general.

CHAPTER 3

Level 5
Leadership

Humility is not a word that is often associated with modern leaders. Indeed, a humble leader is almost a contradiction in terms. It needn't be.

Leading the intellectual charge in praise of humility was C. K. Prahalad, who topped the Thinkers50 ranking in 2007 and 2009 before his premature death in 2010. When we talked with C. K. shortly before his death, he talked about leadership.

What do you think will be the characteristics of the new generation of leaders?
I think humility is a good start. I think we got to a point where people thought that if you wanted to be

a leader, you had to be arrogant. No. First, leadership is about hope, leadership is about change, and leadership is about the future. And if you start with those three premises, I want leaders who are willing to listen because the future is not clear. People can tell you about the past because there's certainty about the past. With the future, there's not much certainty, so you have to listen and bring in multiple perspectives.

Let me use a metaphor. I look at good leaders as sheepdogs. Good sheepdogs have to follow three rules. Number one, you can bark a lot, but you don't bite. Number two, you have to be behind; you cannot be ahead of the sheep. Number three, you must know where to go, and you mustn't lose the sheep.

I always say that because I think that if you think about leadership, it's about consensus building, because when you have stakeholders and you have to worry about co-creation, you must listen and you must build consensus. You can have multiple conversations, but it's the equivalent of barking a lot, but not biting. People who tell you things that are different from what you think may be more valuable than people who agree with you because, as the old saying goes, if you can bark yourself, why have a dog? If all the people you have agree with you, then why do you have so many people? You already know the answer. So dissent is an integral part of understanding what a new leader will look like.

And you must have a point of view about the future. You cannot lead unless you have a point of view. However, most leaders do not have a point of view, or if they have one, they don't express it clearly. Increasing shareholder wealth cannot be a point of view about the future. It's incidental to doing the right things.

So I would say that the leader needs to articulate a point of view on not only where the company can be, but . . . what are the underlying structures of society and how the company is going to participate in and shape that society, and to have a clear understanding of how to build consensus and listen to dissent.

How do you lead from behind? That means a lot of humility.

And finally, I would say that the leaders of the future will have more moral authority. This isn't hierarchical authority. People who come to mind who have tremendous moral authority are people like Gandhi. If you think about Gandhi, he did not have big armies. His force was moral force. And the virtue in Gandhi was that he was never dogmatic. He was tough. He was autocratic many times, but he was willing to change his methods.

And he also said that means are as important as ends; don't take advantage of the British when they have problems. I mean, he could have taken advantage many times. Everybody advised him to take advantage. He said, "No, not this time; we will wait, because means are as important as outcomes." So he had tremendous moral authority. People listened to him.

Now, he was not always the most democratic person, but he listened to a lot of people and he had clear values, which I think is the last thing I want to say. My favorite thought experiment is that if somebody had gone to Gandhi and said, "You declared full *swaraj*, total freedom; why don't we just go and kill 10,000 Brits?" that would have been no go. He would have said, "That is not how we are going to get freedom because there are deep values involved in how we are going to do it." It was nonviolence. It was peaceful resistance, fighting against unjust laws through peaceful means.

And so I think that would be my view of thinking about a leader.

We remember you telling us before that you sometimes contrast Gandhi with General Patton, who was a very different type of leader. Are there any virtues to the Patton style of leadership? How would you characterize that?

Patton's style of leadership had many advantages. But think about it; he was using hierarchical position as a way of demonstrating credibility. Now, he was a very successful general, but if you see the movie, which is always fascinating for me, big American flag and all beautifully dressed up and telling young kids, when you are rocking your grandchild on your knee—I'm paraphrasing—and he asks you, "Grandpa, what did you do during the Great War?" you don't have to say, "I was shoveling shit in some place."

Essentially, what is he saying? I assure you, you will live, don't be afraid. Because what is the worry that a 19-year-old has, a 20-year-old? That he's going to get shot, which many of them did. But he is telling them, "Don't worry, we will win." And he never once used the word *German*. He said, "We'll kill the Huns." And the reason is very simple: there were lots of Germans or soldiers of German extraction in the army.

So Patton was also powerful, but the difference between Gandhi and him is that Gandhi's methods will endure longer. Gandhi said that if we take an eye for an eye, the whole village will be blind. It's a very different way of thinking about it. You don't fight force with force; you fight force with moral authority, and you certainly fight force with logic and consensus building. So it's a different way of resolving conflicts.

I do believe that sometimes we need George Patton, but many times consensus also means conflict resolution. It requires understanding, empathy, time, and patience. So if you think about global peace and stability, it's not at all clear to me that force for force is the right way to go.

So in a funny way, I think that if you start thinking about it, coming to terms peacefully through dialogue and discussion is a safer bet. In fact, I don't know who said this, but anyway, it is an interesting thing. You don't have to make peace with your friends; you only have to make peace with your enemies. So in other words, where people don't agree with you is where you need to talk a lot. Why keep talking to people who all agree with you?

A Blast of Humility

Jim Collins has met more than his fair share of leaders. His research has involved looking at vast numbers of companies to find out what makes some endure and some fall by the wayside, what makes some good, others great, and still others a disaster. It is research that has produced several books, notably *Built to Last* (with Jerry Porras), *How the Mighty Fall*, *Good to Great*, and *Great by Choice* (with Morten Hansen), as well as countless articles.

Built to Last: Successful Habits of Visionary Companies hit the shelves in 1994.[1] The book, which was on the *Businessweek* best-seller list for more than six years, set out to identify the qualities that were essential for building a great and enduring organization, what the authors called "successful habits of visionary companies."

Companies that endure have an effective vision that embodies the core ideology of the organization, which, in turn, has two components: core values (a system of guiding principles and tenets) and core purpose (the organization's most fundamental reason for existence).

Core values, says Collins, are "the organization's essential and enduring tenets—a small set of guiding principles; not to be confused with specific cultural or operating practices; not to be compromised for financial gain or short term expediency."[2]

"Companies that enjoy enduring success have core values and a core purpose that remain fixed while their business strategies and practices endlessly adapt to a changing world," write Collins and Porras.[3]

Prior to *Built to Last*, Collins began a research and teaching career at the Stanford Graduate School of Business. After teaching at Stanford for seven years, he returned to his home town of Boulder, Colorado, and started a management laboratory that ran multiyear research projects, working with senior executives from the public, private, and social sectors. Here he has become "a self-employed professor who endowed his own chair and granted himself tenure." His laboratory examines business issues and structures from a statistical standpoint. "Others like opinions," says Collins. "I prefer data."

Good to Great

In 1996, Collins and his research team turned their attention to another challenging business question: Can a good company become a great company, and, if so, how? Collins figured that if he could take those companies that managed to bridge the divide between good and great and those that had failed to make that leap, then he would be able to separate out the factors that made the difference.

After a five-year research project, Collins had some answers. The team had identified a number of factors that were involved in making a good company great, yet, as Collins noted, the most surprising of these was the type of leadership that was required.

The difference between the good companies and the great companies appeared to come down to different types of leadership. And while Collins may initially have been skeptical that it was possible to attribute such a difference (between good and great) to the style of a single person, his data told him a different story.

Collins introduced a new term to the leadership lexicon to describe this type of leader: Level 5 leadership. Going through the skills at each level, Level 1 is about individual capability, someone who uses his or her knowledge and talent to contribute to the organization. Level 2 is about team skills and working effectively with a group. At Level 3, a person exhibits managerial competence; he or she can get other people organized to work toward shared goals. Level 4 is leadership in the conventional non–Jim Collins sense: the leader articulates a vision and stimulates performance.

The top level is Level 5. Level 5 is the great, while Level 4 leaders are merely good.

Level 5 leaders have all the skills of leaders at the previous four levels, plus something extra: they subordinate the needs of their ego and self-interest to the needs of the organization. Level 5 people have an almost heroic commitment to the company and its mission. The company gets all their emotions—there's no room or energy for self-promotion. The company comes first. But these leaders are never alone. They need a good team with them, and this is something that they are responsible for creating.

When hiring senior executives, organizations should be looking for Level 5 leadership, suggests Collins. But what do these leaders look like, and where do you find them? Well, to start with, they are not outsized personalities or egocentric celebrities.

Indeed, Level 5 leadership challenges the assumption that transforming companies from good to great requires larger-than-life leaders. The leaders that came out on top in Collins's five-year study were relatively unknown outside their industries. The findings appear to signal a shift of emphasis away from the hero and toward the nonhero. Look inside the organization at where there is great performance, but no one is clamoring to be attached to, or associated with, that success.

According to Collins, humility is a key ingredient of Level 5 leadership. His simple formula is Humility + Will = Level 5. "Level 5 leaders are a study in duality," notes Collins, "modest and willful, shy and fearless."[4] These leaders display a number of distinct attributes, says Collins. Although they are instrumental in achieving great results, they never brag about it, preferring to avoid the limelight.

They are resolute about the organization's objectives; however, they do not motivate through force of personality in a charismatic sense, but rather through demonstrating principles and standards. While planning for sustained success, they are happy and even keen to organize an effective succession.

When thing go wrong, these leaders do not pass the buck. Instead, they are happy to shoulder the burden of responsibility. And when things go well, they are quick to praise others and acknowledge the contributions of their team.

When you change your perspective on leadership and adopt a Level 5 view of the world, the organization's talent map changes. Level 5 leaders can be found inside most organizations. The problem is the cult of the hero senior executives that permeates the business world.

"If we allow the celebrity rock-star model of leadership to triumph, we will see the decline of corporations and institutions of all types," says Collins. "The twentieth century was a century of greatness, but we face the very real prospect that the next century will see very few enduring great institutions. If good is the enemy of great—and I believe it is—the current trends in leadership give the decided edge to the enemy."[5]

Leading in Chaos

The modern world is a chaotic place, and not every leader finds the chaos easy to cope with. After *Good to Great*, Collins stumbled upon on another question that intrigued him: How is it that some organizations and leaders can thrive on chaos? Collins took a familiar approach: find companies that can cope well with chaos and that succeed in spite of turmoil, and examine how they differ from those organizations that do not cope so well.

Starting out with 20,400 candidate companies, Collins and his team whittled the list down to just seven; he called these 10X organizations[6] because their performance was at least 10 times better than that of the industry index.

Why were these organizations so successful in a chaotic, fast-paced environment, when other companies were not? A large part of the performance difference was due to leadership, says Collins.

Collins uses the example of Roald Amundsen and Robert Falcon Scott and their journey to the South Pole to illustrate the difference. Both of the teams heading for the South Pole had similar resources and capabilities, and both were operating in a similarly difficult environment. Ultimately, what led to Amundsen's success in reaching the pole first and Scott's failure to do so and perishing on the ice as he returned was a difference in behavior. This difference was very much like the difference between the leaders of 10X companies and those companies that fail to prosper during chaotic times.

The leaders of 10X companies, when faced with a world that they are largely unable to control, seek to exert control over those aspects of it that they can. Collins says that they "embrace a paradox of control and noncontrol." They understand and accept that some aspects of the world are uncertain and uncontrollable, but they refuse to accept the idea that they do not have control over and responsibility for their destiny.

In general, 10X leaders exhibit three behavioral traits, says Collins: "fanatic discipline, empirical creativity, and productive paranoia." Perhaps what is most interesting about Collins's view of the 10X leader in a chaotic world is the concept that he calls 20-Mile Marching. The secret is to make steady, certain progress, consistently hitting performance markers over a long period of time. Thus, if it were possible to push further than the notional "20 miles," whatever target that represented, the leader would hold back. At the same time, however difficult this might be, the leader would always push for a target that was close to the 20-mile mark. These leaders are ambitious, but they have the self-discipline and self-control to hold back.

In Amundsen's case, his team made consistent progress toward its goal, never overdoing it, even in good weather. In contrast, says Collins, Scott's progress was one of stops and starts, overdoing it on good days and stationary on bad days.

On a Level

When we spoke to Jim Collins, we began by asking about Level 5 leadership. He was quick to give a broader perspective.

What can you tell us about Level 5 leadership?
First, let me back up a bit. In general, I have a bias against a CEO-centric view of the world. Leadership answers often strike me as oversimplistic and in dan-

ger of covering up too many variables. If a company
does really well, we say that the reason was great leadership; if it doesn't do well, we say that the leadership
wasn't as great as we thought.

I see leadership as being in our version of the
Dark Ages. In an earlier period, whenever we didn't
understand something—an earthquake or crops failing or disease—we would ascribe it to God. But then
came the Renaissance and the Enlightenment and we
discovered new areas of physics and chemistry, so we
could offer different explanations for earthquakes
and crop failures.

In the twentieth and twenty-first centuries,
when we're looking at the social world, the man-made
world, we are still in the Dark Ages. This is shown by
our predilection for looking for leadership answers.
Leadership is to the twentieth century what God was
to a much earlier period. That doesn't mean that you
have to become an atheist. But if you stop looking for
answers that are always either God or leadership, you
will find other underlying factors.

So how has this view of leadership influenced your research?

In our research, I've always said, let's discount the
role of the leader so that we can find the other factors. Let's assume that there are other things to discover—laws of physics. So going down that path, the
Level 5 leadership finding that came out in *Good to
Great* was not what I expected to find. I didn't even

want to find it. This was not something that we were looking for.

I was very uncomfortable with having a chapter title with the word *leadership* in it. To me this almost felt like a failure, which of course it wasn't. It was good that we had found something interesting.

What the research team said was, we think that the CEOs of these companies had a huge impact on whether they shifted from one level to another, whether they went from the good level to the great level. My reply was that the comparison companies also had leaders, exceptional leaders in many cases, but the companies ended up not performing as well. So you can't say that the answer is leadership, because you have outstanding leaders in both sets of companies. Thus, leadership is not a variable, so go back and do something useful and look for other stuff.

But the research team pushed back at me. They said, "Jim, what we really think you're missing is that you're looking at this as a binary idea—either you are a great leader or you are not, and that's the critical question. But what we believe is that it's much more nuanced than that." That eventually led to the idea that leadership is an evolving series of capabilities and levels of maturity. So it's not a leadership or not question, it's a "what stage of leadership" question and what level of maturity you have reached.

In turn, this led to the insight that those companies that tend to produce the best, most sustained results over time have the characteristics that we put at Level 5, and other companies tend to have leaders who are stuck at Level 4. So the issue wasn't leadership; the real issue was, are you a Level 4 leader, a Level 3 leader, or a Level 5 leader? And that then led to the question, "What are the characteristics of the Level 5 leader?" What cloth were they cut from that made them different from the others?

And what were your conclusions?

That it came down to one essential definition. And the more I live with this definition since the research, which started in 1996, the more comfortable I am with it. The central dimension for Level 5 is a leader who is ambitious first and foremost for the cause— for the company and for the work, not for himself or herself—and has an absolutely terrifying iron will to make good on that ambition. It is that combination— the fact that it's not about the leader, it's not first and foremost for him or her, it's for the company and its long-term interests, of which the leader is just a part. But it's not a meekness; it's not a weakness; it's not a wallflower type. It's the other side of the coin.

Someone who puts the company first?

People who will fire their brother if that is what it takes to make the company great. They will bet the company. They will put their own lives through the worst circumstances, if that is what it takes to make the company great. They will even step away from the CEO role, if that is what it takes to make the company great. They will do whatever it takes. No matter how painful, no matter how emotionally stressing the decision may be, they have the will to do it. It is that very unusual combination that separates out the Level 5 leaders.

Do you intend to broaden your research to the nonprofit and social sector?

Well, as a little preview of my work, I am increasingly interested in the nonbusiness sector. This morning I was working on a big article I'm writing on good to great for the social sector. Eventually I want to do research in which we use the same matched-pair method and apply it to nonprofit health organizations—one that went from good to great and one that didn't.

Ultimately, I believe the greatest contribution of our work is our method. It's actually not our findings. Our findings are just derived from the research method. The question that is of most interest to me is, how do you build a great society? You do it by ensuring that all the component parts of society become great.

If we had a society that only has great companies, we'd have a prosperous society, but we wouldn't have a great society. To be a great society, it isn't enough to have great companies; we must also have great schools and great homeless shelters, and we have to have great orchestras that play great music, and we have to have great healthcare systems.

Ultimately, we have to have great governments, great government agencies, great cities, and great police departments. These are all building blocks of a great society. Personally, it's a question that I find very energizing.

I'm doing a piece of business research now, but it might be the last piece of business research I do. As I work on the good to great social-sector question, I'm really puzzling over the differences between business and the social sector. I'm absolutely convinced that the ideas also apply to the social sector, and in some ways apply even more.

If I can highlight one thing, it's the critical distinction between the business sector and the social or government sector. A big mistake people make is to say that the primary solution to the problems of the nonbusiness sector is for the nonbusiness sector to become more like the business sector. That's the wrong answer. Because what most businesses do, we now know, doesn't correlate with results. And since most businesses are mediocre, why would you want to import the practices of mediocrity? So the real distinction is not between business and social; it's between great and good.

So your ideas are just as relevant for public organizations?

Exactly. Level 5 applies even more in that sort of environment. And it's almost easier to be Level 5 in an organization like the U.K.'s National Health Service because of the passion, because of the cause—people certainly aren't doing it for the money

There's one thing that I would say, and this is really key. Ask yourself, why do so many business executives who move into non–business-related sectors fail? And they often do. In part, it is because being a Level 5 leader in these more social institutions requires a more legislative style of leadership. You are a legislative Level 5 more than an executive Level 5. If you bring a CEO executive style into a legislative setting, where the power is much more diffuse and complex, you will lose. The power will win. Those executives that understand that they need to shift from the executive model to the legislative model, while still being Level 5, tend to have an easier time.

So, then, an exact manifestation would not apply; you wouldn't want to be like the CEOs from *Good to Great*. You want to be a Level 5, but you want to be a legislative Level 5.

Built to Last *has been a big seller for almost a decade. Why?*

I'm continuously surprised to see that the book keeps selling and selling. I think we're pushing 1,000,000 copies in print after some 64 months on the bestseller lists. Why does the topic continue to fascinate readers? My guess is that there are three reasons. First, Jerry and I talked about the corporate icons of the twentieth century; we focused on companies like IBM and Sony and Walt Disney. That draws a lot of people. Second, the quality of our research has obviously stood the test of time; the book uniquely looked at companies both historically (going back to their roots) and comparatively (against their major competitors). Finally, a lot of what's in that book is revelations about humans at work; we weren't afraid to have business findings mixed in with nonbusiness, human findings.

How can we recognize what you call "core values" in an organization?

First of all, you don't need to have explicit core values. They don't have to be pretty, they can even be brutal, and they don't have to be humanitarian, although in most cases they are. The important thing is to know whether the values are believed in effectively. I recommend a test: What values would you continue to hold even if the market, your industry, your customers, and the media penalized you for holding them? Only such values are truly core.

So a company should abandon clients and industries that prevent it from being faithful to its core values, even if those clients and industries are profitable?

Exactly. It's a strong idea that we stated on purpose to make the reader stop and say: "Did I read this right?" Most people think that you need to adjust your values to your strategic needs. Great companies go the other way around: they discard any strategy— no matter how profitable it might be—if it would require actions that are inconsistent with the company's core values.

What about being an innovation leader?

Innovation depends on the company. If we're talking about Sony or 3M, I'll tell you clearly that innovation is a part of their core values, that they didn't read it in a book. It's something that's in their blood and written in their history. But there are other companies that don't value innovation, such as Nordstrom, but this doesn't prevent these companies from having very strong values. Customer intimacy is also a buzzword. It's a strategy concept, not a core value. The point is, there are no "right" core values. The key question is not what are the "right" values, but rather, what are the authentic values.

What about maximizing profits, which is often termed the essence of capitalism? Is that the purpose of a company?

Those who say this are wrong. I am neither a socialist nor the first to say it. In 1954, Peter Drucker, whom I most admire, wrote that maximizing profits is not a reason for business to exist. It is antisocial and immoral. A company doesn't exist to maximize its shareholders' or business owners' profits. Of course it has to worry about earning profits and being profitable. Profits are the blood, oxygen, and nourishment of the company, but the company has to have a deeper purpose. The expression "maximizing profits" is an ideological substitute for the need to find a purpose, something that is sometimes very difficult.

How is it possible to build a visionary organization without a charismatic leader? Business gurus have been trying to sell us the opposite for years.

These gurus are completely wrong. I can give you a list of 20 world-class companies that don't have a charismatic leader. Let me ask you this: where have all these mentors taken this idea of charisma? For me, it is just a twentieth-century version, for the management field, of what an earlier century tried to do by evoking God's name to explain everything. Charismatic leadership is one of the success factors, but there are others. Simplistic, all-purpose answers have to be discarded, like the charismatic leadership one.

So, are there some basic rules for becoming a Built to Last *enterprise?*

First, every company needs to have a core ideology—this is the first component of vision. It is not applied like a cosmetic or copied from somewhere else. It has to be discovered. Having a core ideology means having both core values and core purposes. These are something that remain throughout time.

Then, it is necessary to have a vision of the future, which means defining ambitious goals for the next 10 to 30 years. These goals don't have to be 100 percent manageable; maybe they just have a 50 to 70 percent probability of success. But they'll have impact only if they're described in a lively way, if the images picturing them are clear and motivating enough, if there are passion and conviction.

Finally, aligning vision and implementation is essential. Building a company requires 1 percent vision (without it, nothing matters) and 99 percent alignment of that vision with implementation. Vision provides the context, but alignment allows anyone to understand what the company is about and where it is headed, without having to read papers or brochures, or listening to "top management" speeches. All you have to do is look at the company's operations and actions.

Is Good to Great a sequel?

Actually, I see it as more of a prequel. Ideally, you should read *Good to Great* before you read *Built to Last*. We didn't know it at the time, but the two books, combined, tell the story about how a new company can become a good company, then a great one, then one that is an enduring, visionary company.

But you see "good" as the enemy of great. Why?

Good is the enemy of great. Society doesn't have great schools because we have good schools; we don't have great government because we have good government; and we don't have that many great companies because too many companies are simply good. Ultimately, it's sad but true that many people don't have great lives because they're willing to settle for good lives. To be a great company, you have to adhere to relentlessly stiff standards. You have to stop accepting good-enough behavior and performance. One of the major findings in the new book is that what companies and managers *stop* doing is infinitely more important than what's on their "to do" list.

Is the "greatness gene" embedded in all companies, managers, and employees?

Any company—and I mean *any* organization—can become a great one. That is truly one of my own epiphanies in the last decade. I feel that we learned exactly how good companies become great ones. But the people inside a good company, starting with the leaders, have to commit to this—and stay committed.

CHAPTER 4

The Real Thing

Eye-catching lapses in leaders' ethical standards at the start of the twenty-first century caused a backlash in leadership circles. Corporate leaders, it was argued, had lost touch with ethical standards of behavior and what leadership really entailed. They had lost touch with themselves.

Following the lapses in corporate governance, such as those at Enron, that led to Sarbanes-Oxley, Bill George, then CEO of Medtronic, called for a new type of leader, a more ethical leader, as he put it:

> We realize that the missing ingredients in corpora-
> tions are leaders committed to building authentic

organizations for the long-term. . . . We need authentic leaders, people of the highest integrity, committed to building enduring organizations. We need leaders who have a deep sense of purpose and are true to their core values. We need leaders who have the courage to build their companies to meet the needs of all their stakeholders, and who recognize the importance of their service to society.[1]

George identified a number of attributes that he associated with what he called *authentic leaders,* in particular, values shaped by experience, which provide a moral compass, and complete integrity, which creates trust as well as supplying a sense of purpose for followers/employees.

These ideas were developed much further in George's 2004 book *Authentic Leadership: Rediscovering the Secrets to Creating Lasting Value.*[2] In the book, George refines his thoughts about authentic leaders to determine five qualities that they exhibit and an additional developmental quality that is associated with each of the five qualities.

Thus, according to George, authentic leaders: understand their purpose and have the passion for that purpose that comes from being highly motivated by their work; have solid values, of which integrity should be one, and practice those values, testing themselves in different situations; are able to lead with their heart, treating followers with compassion and firing up employees to achieve great things; can forge a common purpose and build a sense of connectedness so that they develop enduring relationships with, and inspire loyalty and trust from, their employees;

and have a high degree of self-discipline, which means dealing with stress effectively and maintaining their well-being.

Elsewhere, George looked at other leadership-related issues, including how to build an authentic company, performance measurement, governance and ethics, innovation, succession, and leadership at different organizational levels.

Northern Light

In *True North: Discover Your Authentic Leadership* (2007), Bill George and Peter Sims drew on interviews with 125 leaders, aged 23 to 93, selected mainly because of their reputations for authenticity and effectiveness as leaders. At the time, it constituted the largest in-depth study of leadership development. The idea was to learn how these people developed their leadership abilities. Early on, however, the authors noted the following: "Analyzing 3,000 pages of transcripts, our team was startled to see that these people did not identify any universal characteristics, traits, skills, or styles that led to their success."[3]

Instead, George asserts, their leadership abilities emerged from their life stories. "Consciously and subconsciously, they were constantly testing themselves through real-world experiences and reframing their life stories to understand who they were at their core. In doing so, they discovered the purpose of their leadership and learned that being authentic made them more effective," he says.[4]

To begin the journey to authentic leadership, a leader must understand the story of his or her own life. This provides the narrative and the context for authentic leadership, with the person drawing on real-life events to inform his or her leadership today and in the future.

The first capability associated with authentic leadership that George identifies is self-awareness. As George notes, many leaders are so focused on their career development that they neglect the challenging, sometimes painful, introspective exercise required to discover their authentic selves. They also equate success with external measures of success, such as share price, status, titles, money, and fame, without considering whether those measures are truly meaningful for them. Through an honest examination of their lives, leaders become more vulnerable and humane, and less unapproachable and remote.

This also ties in with another facet of authentic leadership, the need to balance extrinsic and intrinsic motivations. That means balancing those external measures of success with intrinsic motivation derived from a sense of the meaning of their lives. Examples include, says George, "personal growth, helping other people develop, taking on social causes, and making a difference in the world."[5] Finding a balance between external and intrinsic motivation is key.

Creating a balanced life is not easy. Leaders have to combine all the different aspects of their lives: their family and friends, their work life and their associates, and their commercial and social lives. George says that leaders need to integrate these different aspects of their lives in such a way that they can be sure that they are the same person in each. This leads to steady and consistent behavior and presence, which, in turn, builds trust.

Authentic leaders work through others to achieve success. So another essential element of authentic leadership is building "extraordinary support teams" to help authentic leaders stay on track. At different times, these teams act as advisors, provide a fresh perspective, give wise counsel, and point out when authentic leaders are heading in the wrong direction. They also provide very welcome comfort and unconditional support when required.

The support team will be drawn from a variety of sources, including family members, close friends, and colleagues. It takes time to build a support network, emphasizes George; such a network starts with one person and accumulates over time. And the relationship has to be two-way, with the leader providing support to the team as well as receiving it.

It is not enough for leaders to go through the process of discovering their authentic leadership style. They must also learn to empower the people around them in their organizations to become leaders in their own right.

Really Real

George was not plowing a lone furrow on authentic leadership. Also adding their voices were the European duo Rob Goffee and Gareth Jones.

Goffee, a professor of organizational behavior at London Business School, and Jones, who was director of human resources and internal communications at the BBC and a senior vice president at Polygram, as well as holding a series of academic positions, began their academic careers as sociologists. "We wanted to change the world and then realized that to do so we first needed to better understand the intricacies of organizational behavior. We worked *in* big corporations and *with* big corporations, encountering restless, brilliant, and often bewildering collections of people," they wrote.

Their early work touched on leadership, but not directly. Their 1998 bestseller, *The Character of a Corporation*, focused on corporate culture, for example.[6] But there were implications for leaders nevertheless. Goffee and Jones took two cultural characteristics, sociability and solidarity. Sociability is about being people-oriented, while solidarity is about all committing to shared objectives. Using a two-by-two matrix approach, they identified four types of organizational culture: networked, mercenary, fragmented, and communal. Each had slightly different implications for leaders.[7]

From this starting point, Goffee and Jones's focus turned to leadership. Their research is resolutely based in the reality of leadership rather than in the leader-as-hero genre. In "Why Should Anyone Be Led by You?," a McKinsey Award–winning article published in 2000, Goffee and Jones note: "You can't do anything in business without followers, and followers in these 'empowered' times are hard to find. So executives had better know what it takes to lead effectively—they just find ways to engage people and rouse their commitment to company goals."[8]

For Goffee and Jones, there were four main qualities that inspiration leaders possessed: they selectively showed their weaknesses, thus appearing more approachable; they relied heavily on intuition in their decision-making processes; they managed employees with "tough empathy"; and they were prepared to reveal where they were different from their followers.

Perhaps one of the most important elements identified by Goffee and Jones, however, was the emphasis on authenticity. As they say,

Of all the facets of leadership that one might investigate, there are few so difficult as understanding what it takes to develop leaders. The four leadership qualities are a necessary first step. Taken together, they tell executives to be authentic. As we counsel the executives we coach: "Be yourselves, more, with skill." There can be no advice more difficult to follow than that.

Over the following few years, Goffee and Jones set out to study this issue, refining their views on leadership as they did so. First, say Goffee and Jones, there are some fundamental truths about leadership that everyone needs to know. One is that leadership is relational, and therefore followers are required if leadership is to exist. And like most relationships, this one needs working at. Leadership is also nonhierarchical. In other words, having a fancy title does not make you a leader. This means that it is possible to be a leader at any level of an organization as long as you have some followers, even if you do not have a fancy job title. For Goffee and Jones, leadership is also contextual—authentic leaders change their behavior to suit the context, while remaining true to themselves.

Leaders need to provide four things in particular for their followers. The first is community: followers want to be part of something. Leaders can connect them to others, and to meaning as part of the organization's purpose. Second, it is essential that leaders convey authenticity to their followers. Employees want to be led by real people, not by people who are behaving the way they think a leader should behave. Followers want their leader to reveal enough of him- or herself so that they can connect with the leader. Third, it is important that followers feel that their efforts are worthwhile and make a difference. Finally, followers want their leader to inspire, enthuse, and excite them, spurring them on to greater achievements and better performance.

In practice, say Goffee and Jones, when leaders are wondering how to be authentic and what authentic leadership requires from them, four things matter most of all. There is an inherent tension between leading according to the context and being authentic, and leaders must master this tension by being highly attuned to the organization. "Only then can you react as an 'authentic chameleon,' adapting effectively to the context without losing your sense of self. Only then can you begin to transform the situation with symbolic actions and decisive behavior to create an alternative, inspiring reality for your followers," say Goffee and Jones.[9]

Self-awareness is an integral part of authentic leadership. But it does not require years of psychoanalysis, say Goffee and Jones. It is about making a connection, knowing what and how much of yourself, your strengths and weakness, and your idiosyncrasies to reveal to others. The authentic leader cannot connect unless she knows her followers well—their hopes, fears, interests, and emotional state. For this, leaders must get close to their followers. At the same time, they may need to challenge or cajole, or even reprimand, the same followers, and so it is useful to know how to create distance in these situations. Finally to convey their vision, yet appear authentic, leaders must choose the medium and the moment that suit their personality and leadership style. And the message must be clear and easy for everyone to understand.

Interestingly, Goffee and Jones also detailed a number of popular conceptions about leadership that they believed were myths. One of those myths, contrary to what many leadership experts argue, is that everyone can be a leader. Not so, say Goffee and Jones. "Many executives don't have the self-knowledge or the authenticity necessary for leadership," they say. And also, many executives don't want to be leaders anyway.

Clever Alternatives

Having refined their model of authentic leadership, Goffee and Jones turned their attention to another thorny issue that many leaders face: how to manage maverick, clever people. Often some of the best innovators and the most productive people in organizations do not want to lead, but neither do they want to be led. That makes life a little difficult for the people who are ostensibly supposed to be leading them and getting them to deliver on the organization's objectives.

All is not lost, say Goffee and Jones, as long as the leader adopts the right approach. Don't tell these clever people what to do; use expert power rather than hierarchy to exert authority. Give the clever people some space to get on with what they do best, but make time to field questions from them, if required, and to ask them questions, too. They are, after all, often cleverer than the boss. Clever people like to be recognized and rewarded, but in ways that they prefer, and especially by people that they value—technical experts in their field, for example. And, of course, the leader must be authentic.

Over the years, we have had many conversations with Goffee and Jones, often in the pubs of London, where they are voluble (in Jones's case) and always interesting company. They met as students of sociology in the 1970s.

Your roots lie in sociology. How did you come to be diverted by leadership?

Jones: We have always been interested in real people doing real jobs. For "Why Should Anyone Be Led by You?," we interviewed a cross section of people. They included a hospital nurse, a Zimbabwean soldier, a head teacher, a round-the-world yachtsman, and a variety of others, as well as many people in an array of corporate positions. We like the approach of the great American broadcaster and writer Studs Terkel. If you engage with people, you learn from them. It doesn't matter where people exercise leadership; they are still leaders.

And that's different from the conventional approach. Leadership has tended to be associated with the heroic and the famous, but our work with companies has exposed us to a variety of leaders who excel at inspiring people. That's what really fascinates us: leaders who succeed in capturing hearts, minds, and souls. Rob and I are fascinated by leadership that, reaching back to the ideas of Max Weber, is antibureaucratic and charismatic. To have leaders with these qualities is not everything in business, but we think that it is worth a lot.

But surely leadership needs some hard-and-fast parameters. It isn't just about attitude and personality.

Goffee: True, leadership is about results. It has to be. Great leadership has the potential to excite people to extraordinary levels of achievement. But it is not only about performance; it is also about meaning. This is an important point—and one that is often overlooked. Leaders at all levels make a difference when it comes to performance. They do so because they make performance meaningful.

And the quest for meaning is increasingly important to societies and individuals. As the pace of change increases, individuals are ever more motivated to search for constancy and meaning. We've become increasingly suspicious of a world dominated by the mere role player.

Jones: In organizations, the search for the meaning and cohesion that leaders provide is increasingly clear. Look at hierarchies. In the old world of organizations, there were ornate hierarchies, more or less stable careers, and clear boundaries. All this has changed. The trouble is that people now realize that hierarchies were not just structural coordinating devices in organizations. Rather, and much more significantly, they were sources of meaning. The organization man, with company blood coursing through his veins, now has to come to terms with a world of high ambiguity in which overidentification with one organization is a problem rather than a career. As hierarchies flatten, meaning disappears, so we look to leadership to instill our organizations with meaning.

This process has been under way for a while. But the corporate scandals of the last few years have brought it into the spotlight. They are a symptom of amoral leadership, and the damage that they have done to the ideology that makes our economic system cohere has been substantial. One side effect of this is that there is a lot of cynicism among executives. If you ask them while they are at work, "What gives your life meaning?," they mouth the latest corporate platitudes. If you ask them at home, they will admit to profound symptoms of meaninglessness as they struggle with work-related stress and dysfunctional family lives.

What's the link between leadership and meaning?

Goffee: If there isn't a clearly articulated purpose, meaning is elusive. Leadership provides that articulation. This search for authenticity and leadership is reinforced whenever we work inside organizations. CEOs tell us that their most pressing need is for more leaders in their organizations—not the consummate role players who seem to surround them. And among those who are lower down in the organization, there is either a plea for more inspiring leadership or, just as common, a fierce desire to develop leadership skills for themselves. Authentic leadership has become the most prized organizational and individual asset.

   Jones: That's what we find when we ask people which set of competences they would most like to develop. They all come up with the same answer: help us to become more effective leaders. They have seen that leadership makes a big difference to their lives and the performance of their organizations. The same is true when we ask CEOs what is the biggest problem they face. They unerringly reply: our organizations need more leaders at every level.

Why are leaders in short supply?

Jones: There are two reasons, we think. First, organizations may desire leaders, but they structure themselves in ways that kill leadership. Far too many of them are machines for the destruction of leadership. They encourage either conformists or role players. Neither makes for effective leaders.

The second reason is that our understanding of leadership is blinkered. For all the research into leadership, it is surprising how little we know about it. We're not criticizing our academic colleagues when we say that, but we are questioning the methods they have used and the fundamental assumptions upon which much of the research has rested.

Goffee: Look at the main leadership literature and you will see that it focuses on the *characteristics* of leaders. There is a strong psychological bias. It sees leadership qualities as being inherent in the individual. The underlying assumption is that leadership is something that we do *to* other people. But in our view, leadership should be seen as something that we do *with* other people. Leadership must always be viewed as a relationship between the leader and the led.

A corollary of this is that books on leadership persistently try to find a recipe for leadership. There are long lists of leadership competences and characteristics. Anyone who reads these books is bound to be disappointed. Reading about Jack Welch isn't going to make you into Jack Welch.

So there are no universal leadership characteristics?
Jones: We don't think so. What works for one leader will not work for another. If you want to become a leader, you need to discover what it is about yourself that you can mobilize in a leadership context.

Do you mean that in order to lead, you need complete self-knowledge?
Jones: That's what a lot of the contemporary writing about leadership suggests. But, while it is undoubtedly very useful to have a great deal of emotional intelligence, for example, none of the leaders we have talked to or worked with have had full self-knowledge. Life and leadership aren't like that.

Goffee: What they do have is an overarching sense of purpose, together with *sufficient* self-knowledge to recognize their potential leadership assets. They don't know it all, but they know *enough*.

Jones: That might sound a bit too pragmatic, but it is actually based on recognizing three fundamental axioms about leadership. The first of these is that leadership is *situational*. What is required of the leader will always be influenced by the situation. Think of Rudy Giuliani in the wake of September 11 or of Winston Churchill. In organizational life, hard-edged, cost-cutting turnaround managers are often unable to offer leadership when there is a need to build.

Our second observation is that leadership is *nonhierarchical.* Reaching the top of an organization does not make you a leader. Hierarchy alone is neither a necessary nor a sufficient condition for the exercise of leadership.

Goffee: You could argue that the qualities that take you to the top of large-scale and often highly political organizations are not obviously the ones associated with leadership. People who make it to the top do so for a whole variety of reasons—including political acumen, personal ambition, time serving, and even nepotism—rather than real leadership quality.

So leadership is not the sole preserve of the chosen few.

Goffee: No. Great organizations have leaders at all levels. Successful organizations—whether they be hospitals, charities, or commercial enterprises—seek to build leadership capability widely and to give people the opportunity to exercise it.

Jones: The third pillar of our view of leadership is that leadership is *relational.* Put simply, you cannot be a leader without followers. Leadership is a relationship that is built actively by both parties. This web of relationships is fragile and requires constant re-creation.

This doesn't mean that everything is always harmonious. It isn't. There may be an edge in a relationship, but that's because effective leaders know how to excite their followers to become great performers.

What are the implications—at a very practical level—for those who aspire to leadership? What do they need to know and do?

Jones: The answer is simple, deceptively simple, in fact: to become a more effective leader, you must *be yourself, more, with skill.*

First, to be a leader you must *be yourself.* Look at Sir Richard Branson, the Virgin boss, and the way he uses his physical appearance—casual dress, long hair, and a beard—to convey the informality and nonconformity that have become a central part of his leadership and, indeed, of the Virgin brand. Followers want to be led by a person, not a role holder, a position filler, or a bureaucrat.

The leaders we studied were very adept at deploying their differences in ways that attract followers. Richard Branson's differences *signify* a message; they are *authentic*, not falsely manufactured; and they are *seen* by others. We are talking, then, not of just *any* personal difference, but of an artful and authentic display, often fine-tuned over many years, of genuine differences that have the potential to excite others.

Goffee: The link between self-knowledge and self-disclosure is a central—and increasingly fashionable—starting point for understanding effective leadership. But it is not everything. Leaders must be themselves *in context.* Great leaders are able to read the context and respond accordingly. They tap into what exists and bring *more* to the party. In management jargon, they add value. This involves a subtle blend of authenticity and adaptation, of individuality and conformity.

The thing about effective leaders is that they do not simply react to context. They also shape it by conforming *enough*. This is the *skill* element. It involves knowing when and where to conform. Without this, leaders are unlikely to survive or make the connections they need in order to build successful relationships with others. To be effective, the leader needs to ensure that his or her behaviors mesh sufficiently with the organizational culture to create traction. Leaders who fail to mesh will simply spin their wheels in isolation from their followers.

Can you explain what you mean by conforming enough?

Goffee: Leaders who succeed in changing organizations challenge the norms—but rarely all of them, all at once. They do not seek out instant head-on confrontation without understanding the organizational context. Indeed, survival (particularly in the early days) requires measured adaptation to an ongoing, established set of social relationships and networks. To change things, the leader must first gain at least minimal acceptance as a member—and the rules for early survival are rarely the same as the rules for longer-term success.

Jones: If you look around the corporate world, there have been countless examples of CEOs who rode roughshod over organizational contexts. Sometimes they have reaped short-term gains. But, in the long term, sustainable change requires the leader to understand and tune in to the organizational context. Having done so, the leader can instigate change with credibility and with a greater chance of success. Ignore this, and the results can be disastrous. Think of Al Dunlap or the host of ruthless downsizers and asset strippers who conspicuously fail to deliver long-term change.

Goffee: The question is: Who can read organizations well, and how do they develop this skill? Clearly, some leaders are able to read situations intuitively largely as a result of many years' experience in different contexts. They develop a kind of wisdom that makes them less dependent on conceptual models to give them insight or even to guide their interventions. But are there universal principles that underlie organizational relationships and that might frame the possibilities for change? We think there are. Our consulting work suggests that many people find models that refine their context-reading skills.

We have developed a way of understanding organizational context that is based on a view of organizations as communities. In our model, which draws heavily on classic sociology, there are two key cultural relationships: sociability and solidarity. Sociability refers primarily to affective relations between individuals who are likely to see each other as friends. They tend to share ideas and values and to associate with each other on equal terms. At its heart, sociability represents a relationship that is valued for its own sake. It is usually initiated through face-to-face contact, although it may be maintained through other forms of communication, and it is characterized by high levels of mutual help. No real conditions are attached.

Solidarity, by contrast, describes task-focused cooperation between individuals and groups. It does not depend on close friendship or even personal acquaintance, nor does it need to be continuous. It arises only from a perception of shared interest—and, when this occurs, solidarity can produce intense focus.

Although this discussion may seem a little abstract, sociability and solidarity relationships are actually all around us—in our families, sports teams, social clubs, and communities. Arguably, this ubiquity is what drew the attention of the early sociologists in the first place. In effect, we all have an interest in—and are affected by—these relationships. Ask someone to describe his or her ideal family, for example, and typically that person will tell you it is one in which the members like and love one another (that's the sociability element) and that pulls together when times get tough (that's solidarity).

There are a lot of tensions and paradoxes at work here. The leader needs to be incredibly sensitive.

Jones: Yes, there are a lot of tensions. Leaders must reveal strengths, but show weaknesses; be individuals, but conform enough; establish intimacy, but keep their distance. Managing these tensions lies at the heart of successful leadership.

That's quite demanding. Wouldn't it be easier to imitate Jack Welch?

Goffee: The trouble is that even if that were possible, what works for Jack Welch won't work for you.

Our experience suggests that excellence in one or two of these areas we've talked about is insufficient for truly inspirational leadership. It is the interplay among these areas, guided by situation sensing, that enables great leaders to find the right style for the right moment. In other words, every leader is unique.

Jones: And leadership is uniquely difficult. There is no point pretending that leadership is straightforward. Anyone who has ever been in a leadership position will tell you that it is complicated, demanding, and full of personal risk. Clearly, not everyone can be a leader, and there are many very talented individuals who are simply not interested in shouldering the responsibility of leadership. To assume that everyone has the sheer energy, drive, and willpower required to offer inspirational leadership to others is facile. We argue that each individual has unique differences that potentially can be exploited in a leadership role. So, each of us has to address the blunt question: Do I want it? And if I do, do I want it enough to put in the work required and make the necessary sacrifices?

Goffee: And then if you take on a leadership role, you have to ask: *Why should anyone be led by you?* Why should *we* be led by you? Effective leaders must answer these questions every day in everything they say and do. Otherwise, the shortage of leaders will continue, as their practice of leadership will be fatally flawed.

The Leader's Mind

Authenticity is a reassuring concept. Surely we can all be ourselves. But getting at its heart is surprisingly difficult. Sincerity and insincerity, truth and falsity, genuineness and artifice are all matters of judgment—and taste. Liz Mellon of Duke Corporate Education and author of *Inside the Leader's Mind: Five Ways to Think Like a Leader*, offers a different perspective on authenticity in leadership.

Why focus on the leader's mind?

I had been in the business for a long time, and had spent such a lot of time in the classroom or in coaching sessions with leaders, and one question kept coming up again and again. It was really about authenticity.

How do I follow my company or organization's view of the excellent leader—its list of leadership attributes or competencies? How do I follow that and still be an authentic leader? How can I still be, in essence, me as well as the corporate leader they want me to become?

What did that tell you?

It told me that we are missing something. In our drive to observe and measure how our leaders behave, we are missing something very important.

It's about how leaders think. When you get to behavior, there's such a huge range of different ways in which leaders can behave that when you try to capture it in a list, it is difficult. That's why leaders struggle. They look at the big list and wonder where they are on it.

But how we think, how we see a situation, how we conceptualize our job, how we believe the world works—that's what drives our behavior. So where leaders are is based on how they think about themselves and about their job.

You describe five ways of thinking like a leader.

Yes, but the first thing to say is that they don't go in any order. It's not, "Right, first I'll do this, then I'll do this." It's more like dance steps. You know the steps are there, but the music and the pace will depend on you, the individual. So, how you get there varies.

One of the five ways of thinking is called No Safety Net. What does that mean?

That means that someone has to step out because he or she is the leader. Everyone expects the leader to be the first one to step out—over the precipice, over the abyss, with nothing below him. The leader is the one doing the balancing act. There is no safety net; he has to step out. He has to be that brave.

When I talk to the people I interviewed and ask what No Safety Net means, they describe it as a way of thinking: "It means that I have to be the first one out there. I'm taking the first step. I'm taking the risk. I'm the one who does that."

However, when I ask them for examples of how they do that, I get a huge range of responses about behaviors.

What other types of thinking are there?

Another one that's at the very personal level is Comfortable in Discomfort. There's a whole lot of ambiguity and complexity out there in the world. Imagine that you are running a business that spans multiple countries, has thousands of employees, and faces all the complexity that goes with that: markets, politics, national cultures.

Somehow you have to live with that, find a way through it, and still have the courage to take the decisions that need to be taken, while being comfortable with the level of complexity that's coming at you.

That manifests itself in different ways. Sometimes the leader has tons of data to support her decision making: whether she should go into China or divest Sri Lanka or whatever the decision that she is considering may be, but she waits because she just knows that the timing isn't right. Or maybe there are no data at all, and the leader makes a decision to go in a certain direction.

For leaders who are coping with that kind of complexity, it must be difficult not to convey the pressure that they have to deal with to their employees.

Exactly. The leaders have to live with that uncertainty, and with a smile on their face, so that they are not worrying everybody else around them with the level of ambiguity they are actually coping with, day in and day out.

That brings me to a way of thinking that I call I Am the Enterprise: thinking very carefully about the message you're sending out to others. A good illustration of this is Tom Albanese, the former CEO of Rio Tinto. In the space of a few years, among other things, he faced a hostile takeover, bought a company almost the same size as Rio Tinto, and entered the Chinese market. He faced a huge amount of complexity and ambiguity, and he had to be always on.

And he told me a really interesting anecdote. Coming out of one of the more fraught meetings during that period, he looked at his assistant and realized that she was looking a little bit worried. So he said to her, "I know I've got to be smiling, but actually you have to be, as well; otherwise they'll think I've told you something that's worrying you."

So at an enterprise level, and in running the organization, there is that way of thinking where the leader is always aware of the message that he and his team are sending out.

What about the way of thinking that you style On My Watch?

This occurs at the organization level. It is a really interesting way of thinking. The image I have in my mind here is that you are crossing the Atlantic on a yacht, following the trade winds, and you are the one who has got to stay awake for the night. Everyone else on the boat is asleep.

On My Watch means that, for a period of time, you have that incredibly enhanced sense of responsibility. You know that somebody took the watch before you, that you're on for this watch, and that you're then going to hand the responsibility over to somebody else. So you have to be able to take care of three time zones: the past, the present, and the future.

The problem with running a business is that today is so busy, so hectic, and so preoccupying that there is a danger that you will spend all your time thinking just about today. That won't help you create a different tomorrow.

Dennis Nally, the global chairman of PricewaterhouseCoopers (PwC), told me an interesting story. He said that when he was younger, he used to just worry about his results today, because that was when he was making his reputation. When he was promoted to CEO of PwC in the United

States, and then to global chairman, he realized that his job was to worry about the things that he is doing today that may not be creating any value today, but that lay the foundations for somebody else to be famous in the future. That humility was really very interesting.

Not only do leaders have to stop doing what they're doing today in order to gaze into the future, but they also have to understand and respect the past, and to know which bits to keep and honor and which bits to discard and when.

Exactly. I think one of the reasons that some leaders are very poor at leading change is that they arrive with their 100-day plan and draw a line in the sand, and it is often along the lines of, "Let's discard the past; that was then, this is now; off we go."

But you're addressing thousands, maybe hundreds of thousands, of people who've invested years of their life in creating where you are today. When the leader shows them her vision of the brave new world, they are likely to say, "Well, wait a moment. I'm not sure I want a part of that. I'm not sure you see me as part of that."

So reverence for the past is really important; you need to integrate that story into a future. Yet you have to remember that if the past is going to stop you from moving to the future, you have to gently leave it behind—but to do so gently.

And that brings us to authenticity?

Yes. Authenticity is absolutely integral to this. I call it the Solid Core, and like many of the other thinking styles, it is multifaceted. This is a tumultuous world, full of information and technology and change. Look across the globe; there are events like the tsunami in Japan and huge companies going bust that you would never expect. In this maelstrom of communication, somehow you have to go inside yourself and say, "This Solid Core is my compass, and this will give me a sense of where I need to go."

That is about being authentic. That's where I think the heart of authenticity lies. It is in having this core of inner certainty. I don't know where it comes from, and, actually, neither do the CEOs. Some of them say, "I've been in this industry for 25 years, 30 years, so it's all that experience."

Dennis Nally said, "Actually, I've been this way since I was 15. I've always had this inner sense." Sim Tshabalala, the group deputy chief executive officer of Standard Bank Group, said that for him, it's about his values, and one of his values involves using the platform of business to build society, in this case first South Africa and then Africa more broadly.

So it's a complex concept, but they all have it. They all have this core of authenticity that surrounds the way they approach life and their work.

So, having formulated this set of ways of thinking, you then took them out and discussed them with a range of leaders, and they seemed to resonate with those leaders?

They did. We have observed leaders in action and derived these principles, and now we are applying them back. So it's really grounded in practice, in what leaders really do.

These five ways of thinking really resonated. I can barely get through them before people say, "Oh, yes," and tell us a story that relates to one of them.

So there are leaders who think like this. We don't know how or why, or when they began thinking like this. But what about the rest of us who want to be leaders? Can we learn these ways of thinking?

That's where it comes back to authenticity. Some leaders would say that they have always thought like that. But others have said that they learned. Comfortable in Discomfort is a good example. Jacko Maree, the former group CEO of Standard Bank, said to me that he was Comfortable in Discomfort, but he had not used to be 20 years ago. He learned this one; it came with maturity.

So the good news is that these ways of thinking can be learned. For aspiring leaders everywhere, these ways of thinking can be embraced and learned.

Charisma and the Dark Side

*C*harisma is a Greek word meaning "gift." In the New Testament, *charisms* were gifts bestowed by the Holy Spirit. These charismatic gifts included wisdom, knowledge, faith, or the ability to perform miracles or speak in tongues; they also included gifts that were intended to be used to organize and build the church.

Max Weber, the German sociologist, philosopher, and political economist, took up the notion of charisma as a source of authority and legitimacy. He used it to describe a situation in which authority is derived not from rules or position, but instead from a "devotion to the specific and exceptional sanctity, heroism, or exemplary character of an individual person, and of the normative patterns or order revealed or ordained by him."[1]

In Weber's view, charisma was associated with times of crisis. People in trouble look to charismatic leaders, with their characteristic sense of mission and destiny, their zeal and purpose, to lead them to safety.

The nature and characteristics of charisma have been investigated by sociologists and political scientists for many years. Characteristics variously associated with charismatic leaders have included such things as an overarching vision and ideology, heroic acts, and the ability to inspire. Some researchers held the view that charismatic leadership was a relational concept and was dependent on the perspective of followers.

However, while charisma has been long associated with military and political leaders, such as Napoleon, Churchill, and Gandhi, it did not really feature significantly in the studies of management and organizational theorists until the 1980s.

"Charisma wasn't always as important in business as it is today," notes Harvard Business School professor Rakesh Khurana. "For three decades following World War II, . . . the typical CEO was an organization man who worked his way up the ranks."[2]

According to Khurana, that started to change in 1979 with the appointment of Lee Iaccoca as CEO of Chrysler. "Iacocca was inspirational in a way that previous business leaders had not been. His successful turnaround of Chrysler made him a national hero in America and ushered in the era of the charismatic CEO."

Leadership theorist Jay Conger was one of the first to propose a framework for studying charisma in the organizational context. In doing so, he set out to "strip the aura of mysticism" from charisma. Instead of considering charisma to be some sort of magical superpower, he envisaged it as a behavioral process.

By treating charisma as something that is attributed to one person by others, it becomes possible to dissect those behaviors that merit such an attribution. Conger suggested that there are a number of behavioral components of charismatic leadership, although he also stressed that all the components are interrelated and form a "constellation of components."

The components operate within a three-stage process of charismatic influence. Initially, the executive leader has to assess the existing situation and decide what resources are required and what obstacles to progress there are. He or she must also take a look at the members of the organization and gauge their needs and their level of satisfaction. During this phase, charismatic leaders need to be *highly sensitive to their environment*, both social and physical. This enables them to form an accurate assessment of both the environmental constraints and the resources required to achieve their goals, and the state of mind of the members of the organization. An accurate assessment is critical, as charismatic leaders often embark on risky and radical courses of action, and they need to be sure that they can take everyone else with them.

Another behavioral component that is present at this stage is the ability to recognize flaws and deficiencies in the existing system. Charismatic leaders "*actively search out existing or potential shortcomings in the status quo.*" Because they home in on, and are intolerant of, these shortcomings, they are seen as organizational reformers, agents of change.

The second phase of charismatic influence is the formulation and conveyance of the goals set by the leader. Charismatic leaders are different from other leaders both in the type of goals that they set and in the way that they tell others about those goals.

Conger suggested that the charismatic leader has *future vision*, and that this both is usually strategic in nature, idealized, and substantially different from the status quo, and represents an embodiment of the perspective shared by the members of the organization.

In order to convey this vision, the charismatic leader needs to be a credible communicator, and here *likableness* is important. Such leaders need to be able to be, or appear to be, "a likable, trustworthy, and knowledgeable person," said Conger.

Finally, for the purposes of formulating the goals and disseminating them, *articulation* is an essential component. The charismatic leader must articulate both the current and future situation and his or her motivation for leading. As they do this, charismatic leaders are careful to emphasize the positive elements of their future vision and the negative elements of the status quo.

Charismatic leaders communicate through both verbal and nonverbal means. Thus, dress, gestures, actions, use of language, rhetoric, and high energy all form part of the charismatic leader's messaging.

In the last stage of charismatic influence, the leader shows how the organization can achieve the goals that he or she has articulated and that are shared by all the members of the organization. To do this, such a leader needs to demonstrate *trustworthiness*. Charismatic leaders obtain the trust of their followers by translating their dissatisfaction with the status quo and the goals that will deliver their vision into *behavior* that appears to have a high risk of personal loss or loss of position or status. Such leaders demonstrate their selfless dedication to the cause by relentlessly focusing on their goals and engaging in actions that involve considerable risk to themselves. The greater the risk, the greater the trust and the greater the charismatic effect.

All that remains is for charismatic leaders to show that they have some relevant knowledge and expertise, past and present, in the areas that they are seeking to influence. They do this by pointing out the technological and other inadequacies of the status quo, as well as devising strategies and unconventional tactics to achieve their objectives.

Saviors and CEOs

Research by Harvard Business School's Rakesh Khurana noted that the impact that CEOs actually have on companies is less than is commonly believed. Khurana estimated that anywhere from 30 to 40 percent of a company's performance is attributable to industry effects, 10 to 20 percent to cyclical economic changes, and perhaps just 10 percent to the CEO.[3] Khurana went on to challenge the business world's obsession with star CEOs in *Searching for a Corporate Savior: The Irrational Quest for Charismatic CEOs*.[4]

Speaking with Khurana, we began by asking what his research suggested about the importance of leaders.

> *Are you suggesting that leaders simply do not matter?*
> My intention was to say that when it comes to economic performance, leaders don't matter in the way we understand them to matter, not to dismiss leadership completely out of hand.
>
> Unlike that today, little of the classical research on leadership focuses on how to dissect the performance

of companies. Our predecessors had a more sophisticated understanding of the relationship between organizations and performance. Over the last 20 years, we have made simplistic connections between individual leadership and performance outcomes.

Classical leadership theory is also more sophisticated about what leaders do in organizations. It doesn't support the kind of egotistical notion that has emerged over the last 20 years, but rather takes the view that leaders in organizations actually play a role in creating meaning for their participants. That includes for-profit organizations.

So are you suggesting that the leader's role is not a superficial, image-related one, but something far deeper?

There is more to leadership than the type of pseudo-charismatic leadership where the PR department, the media, and the CEO actively participate in creating an image of charisma.

In fact, leaders create the conditions for people to derive meaning from their institutions. They do it in a way where the impact is not directly seen in ROI, for example, but rather comes from a variety of other activities and actions.

So, for example, we often focus on a leader's ability to uphold the organization's values through his or her own behaviors and actions. The leader makes architectural decisions that allow people to derive a great deal of meaning from their work—by ensuring that the work has variety and autonomy and provides feedback, for example. The leader creates meaning by paying attention to hiring and retaining individuals who behave in a way that is consistent with the organization's explicit values and purpose. Those are really important types of actions that don't manifest themselves in the next quarter's reports.

The leadership model of the last 20 years seems to have a lot of flaws. Is a new kind of leadership needed for the modern age?
I think we do need a new model of leadership. I would call it *institutional leadership*.

Institutional leadership is absolutely critical in contemporary society. We have to understand that many individuals in society have latent talents. People are unaware of their true potential. Leaders need to be able to tap into that potential.

Leaders should understand that many of the institutions they lead were created to solve a certain set of problems and issues in society. Leaders may be quite gifted when it comes to understanding and solving those problems personally. However, they must also create and institutionalize a process by which leadership is distributed throughout the organization, so that it can be carried on in their absence. It is that kind of leadership that we have to find again.

And so what I mean by institutional leadership is changing and transforming an organization beyond its utilitarian function—infusing it with a sense of purpose and with values that are consistent with the larger values of the society.

What role must these future leaders play?

The task of the leader in the future involves a variety of factors. But institutional leaders, in particular, must find abilities, set goals, reaffirm sacred values, and motivate individuals toward those high values.

In contrast, many business students look at the scorecard of stock price as an indication of whether someone is a good leader or not. That's a very narrow, almost cynical way of understanding the importance of leadership in business. I believe that business is an honorable way of life when people are willing to question the most cherished assumptions.

Ultimately, businesses and business leaders have to be judged not simply by the gain in the stock price, but by qualities such as honor, self-restraint, and the kind of values that are often associated with institutional leadership, as opposed to individualistic leadership.

So how should we assess the performance of institutional leaders?

By asking questions like: During a person's leadership, did he or she increase or decrease constituents' trust in that institution? During that person's reign, did he or she serve as a symbol for others, in terms of representing the kinds of values that we want our institutions to articulate and represent? Did he or she renew the system in a way that allowed that institution to be better aligned to its challenges?

What do effective leaders actually do?

They lead by sharing power, by spreading initiative and responsibility. They resolve tensions and conflicts that paralyze organizations and prevent them from realizing larger objectives. They create and identify resources that allow the group effort to be carried out. It is very difficult to describe. Leadership is a very complex social process. Inevitably, any kind of discussion like this makes it seem more orderly than it really is.

Leaders make decisions; they act on them; they realize that those decisions are right or wrong. In some cases, they revise them; in other cases, they reverse them. Misunderstandings are frequent.

What about the followers? Where do they fit into the leadership equation?

It is important to understand the complex interplay between the leaders and those who are led. I always believe that good followers produce good leaders. And in some ways, whom we choose as our leaders tells us a lot about our society.

We should talk about the failures of followership. While we have focused on the failures of leadership in the last couple of years, there still needs to be a discussion about the failures of followership.

I agree with Hegel, who said, and I'm paraphrasing here, tragedy is not the result of evil triumphing over good, but the result of two partial goods trying to impose their will on each other.

There still appears to be a tension between leadership for short-term gain and leadership with a long-term strategy.

The reason it feels like a tension is that often there is no clear articulation of where leaders are trying to take their organizations. If you have a clear purpose and set of goals, everyone can understand it, and it can be articulated to its various constituents. Then a leader can explain the kinds of decisions he or she is making inside the organizations to achieve those goals and that purpose. And people tend to be very patient.

But if you really pushed and pressed certain corporate leaders on what the strategy of their organization is, what its purpose is, and what they are trying to get done, they would have a hard time getting much further than platitudes about shareholder value or pleasing the customer. Those kinds of platitudes don't offer a clear direction, so it is hard to articulate the logic behind them. You need to have very clear articulation, and that requires having a good sense of the environment and knowing what it is you are trying to get done. You need to be able to articulate that to your constituencies, like shareholders or resource providers, and it is that clarity that helps.

What are the big challenges ahead concerning leadership?

Trying to figure out how to preserve some of the benefits of nimbleness and individuality that we have seen over the last few years, and at the same time transform our leadership and our institutions to become more responsible toward society at large.

To recall that the ends that leaders serve have to do with things like ensuring a healthy, vibrant society; creating context that takes advantage of people's individual initiatives; and leading an increasingly divergent world, with divergent points of view, toward a common shared purpose.

Those are very complicated challenges. But that is the way things need to go. We are trying to figure out how to preserve the good and at the same time get rid of the dangers and the excesses.

A Walk on the Dark Side

Charismatic leaders, through their ability to carry people with them toward a shared objective, can achieve great things in organizations. But the power that they derive from charisma can also be misused. Set on the wrong course, charismatic leaders can prove highly destructive.

A spate of corporate misdemeanors toward the end of the 1990s and the beginning of the 2000s prompted new questions about leadership and charisma. Bernie Ebbers at WorldCom and Dennis Kozlowski at Tyco were both charismatic leaders who led organizations to their downfall. The collapse of Enron was also fueled by a heady cocktail of charisma and greed. Right up until the very end, former CEO Jeffrey Skilling and CFO Andrew

Fastow continued to charm investors and analysts at gatherings that one insider likened to revival meetings.

Conger was some way ahead of the curve when he drew attention to the "shadow side of leadership" in his book *Charismatic Leadership in Organizations*, coauthored with Rabindra N. Kanungo.[5] Conger and Kanungo distinguished between negative and positive forms of charismatic leadership, based on the extent to which the leader's goals and activities are self-serving rather than altruistic.

Charismatic leaders who take the dark side are egotistical and controlling, desire personal power and achievement, are secretive, use whatever means they have available to obtain or enforce compliance, and are unethical. Quite often a bad charismatic leader will select a vision that suits his or her personal needs and subvert the energy and effort and resources of his or her followers to achieve those ends.

In her 2004 book, *Bad Leadership: What It Is, How It Happens, Why It Matters*,[6] Barbara Kellerman noted that effective leadership and bad leadership are not necessarily incompatible. You can be highly effective and still be a bad leader.

People will follow bad leaders for much the same reasons that they follow good leaders. Bad leaders, for a time at least, provide order and structure, safety, simplicity, and certainty. They articulate attractive visions and organize and carry out collective work.

Bad leaders can be broadly divided into two categories: ineffective leaders and unethical leaders. Ineffective leaders fail to get things done. They are characterized by "missing traits, weak skills, strategies badly conceived, and tactics badly employed." Ineffective leaders may set admirable objectives, but lack the means to achieve them.

Add ineffective followers to ineffective leaders and you have a potent force for futility. The most effective followers "think for themselves, self-direct their work, and hold up their end of the bargain. They continuously work at making themselves integral to the enterprise, honing their skills and focusing their contributions and collaborating with their colleagues." Ineffective followers do none of this; they are weak and dependent, and do not commit or contribute to the group.

As for unethical leaders, they are aware of what is right but choose to proceed in another direction. Good leadership is usually associated with ethical leadership. James MacGregor Burns offered three characteristics of ethical leaders: they put followers' needs before their own, they embody virtues such as courage and honesty, and they exercise leadership in the interest of the common good. Bad leaders can be either ineffective, unethical, or both.

Bad leaders, says Kellerman, come in seven types. *Incompetent leaders* lack the "will or skill (or both) to sustain effective action." In addition, they can be incompetent in many ways. They can be stupid, lack emotional intelligence, be chaotic, or be lazy.

Flexibility is often touted as a key characteristic of successful organizations. Leaders too benefit from being adaptable and able to cope with new situations. The *rigid leader*, therefore, is usually a bad leader. Rigid leadership occurs when the leader and some, if not all, followers are inflexible and unyielding. They may be competent, but they are not adaptable. We all know examples of leaders who persist in pursuing the same course of action just because it has led to success before, even though circumstances have changed and that previously successful response is no longer effective.

Good leaders learn to temper their excesses. A leader who is ruled by his or her urges is a bad leader. *Intemperate leaders* lack self-control, and this is compounded by having followers who are unwilling or unable to intervene.

Some leaders like to lead, but don't care about the people that they lead. They have no interest in the needs, desires, and hopes of their followers, or of other people that they come into contact with.

What selfish leaders do care about, though, is furthering their own ends. They focus on achieving their own objectives and are quite happy to trample on other people in order to get there. The selfish leader's needs come first; everything else comes second. Kellerman calls this type of leader the *callous leader*— unkind and uncaring, ignoring or overlooking the needs, wants, and wishes of other members of the group or organization.

Some leaders are just plain *crooked*. In recent years, a spate of corporate scandals has exposed a sizable number of rotten apples. Why are some leaders corrupt? It is the age-old reason that has motivated bad leaders for centuries. Usually, says Kellerman, it is because they are greedy—for power, money, or some other scarce resource.

And, in an increasingly results-driven world, where reward is closely tied to performance, which in turn is measured against set criteria, the temptation to cheat is ever present. Bribery and corruption is not a new phenomenon, admittedly. Roman emperors were grand masters of questionable practices, for example. But if corrupt leaders lie, cheat, steal, and put self-interest ahead of the public interest, then clearly they fail to conform to the ethical component required of good leadership.

Burying your head in the sand or conveniently looking the other way isn't great leadership, either. If something is outside the group, the organization, or their sphere of direct responsibility, *insular leaders* are not interested. They disregard the health and welfare of their followers. It's the leadership equivalent of shrugging one's shoulders and saying, "It's nothing to do with me."

And then there is *evil leadership*. What defines evil leadership? Deriving satisfaction from hurting others is one definition of evil. Evil leaders not only terrorize but seek to prolong suffering. With evil leadership, the leader and at least some followers commit atrocities. Pain is used as an instrument of power. The psychological or physical harm caused is severe rather than slight.

While some leaders are incontrovertibly bad, many fall into a gray area. It is not always possible to decide whether a leader is good, bad, or indifferent. Indeed, the same leader may be all three at different times.

Is it important to consider the nature of bad leaders? Kellerman believes that by knowing what constitutes bad leadership and followership, we can seek to avoid it.

Smart Fails

Of course, statistically, the bad leadership apples are a very small sample of the leadership population—even in politics. For other leaders, however, the best intentions can lead to disaster. Syd Finkelstein of the Tuck Business School at Dartmouth College is the author of *Why Smart Executives Fail*, among other bestsellers.[7] Upbeat and personable, failure seems an unlikely subject for Finkelstein's focus. We began our discussion with the $64 million question.

So, why do smart executives fail?

When you dig down into what's behind it all, it's really all about people and how people make decisions or nondecisions. To a large extent, it's about how people behave. When you're running a company, the margin for error is usually a lot narrower than it is in everyday life.

Behaviors like not wanting to acknowledge that the world is changing around you; procrastinating; sticking your head in the sand; avoiding feedback, especially negative feedback; and surrounding yourself with people who think you are great can really come back and bite you.

What about all the examples of great leaders we get to read about in articles and books?

People get a little get tired of seeing all these books from CEOs about how great they were, ignoring all the things that didn't go so well.

And then you have the consultants' books that look at maybe 10 different client experiences, all of which tell you to take a certain course of action. But what they miss is the hundreds of other companies that may have failed doing exactly the same thing.

In a way, a modern example of that is Steve Jobs. When people hear me and some of the things I talk about related to humility, open-mindedness, and adaptability, one out of every two or three times somebody will say, "I hear what you're saying, but Steve Jobs didn't do any of that; I read the book." (This was especially true when Steve was still alive.)

And that's right. He didn't do any of that. But if you want to create a theory of leadership based on Steve Jobs, you're going to have a sample size of one. And I'm quite convinced that 99 out of 100 people that adopt that management and leadership style are going to fail. The reason I'm quite convinced of this is that it's similar to the failing CEOs I looked at.

So it's easy to fall into the trap of looking at an exception, or a couple of great success stories, because they get a lot of publicity and people read about it. But you miss out on where the real action is.

If you really care about how organizations work, how people make decisions, and how leaders think, you need to have a much more diverse sample. That's the importance of looking at not just what's right, but what's wrong.

Leaders should learn from the bad as well as the good? When my book first came out, *Businessweek* wrote an article—not a review of the book, but an article— about me, how I teach, and the subject.

What the author thought was so intriguing was that I was teaching about what goes wrong in places like business schools, where people spend all their time looking at the best practices rather than the worst practices.

In fact, you need a combination of both. There is a fair amount of research that shows that diversity or diverse perspectives or variance in experience leads to the better training of individuals in a lot of walks of life.

Are leaders learning, do you think? Is there a sense that they are more grounded in reality?
It varies across industries. In general, while there is much more awareness of what can go wrong when a leader adopts the imperial CEO view of the world, it's hard to act upon that awareness. If it were easy, everybody would do it.

To get to the top of an organization, you've got to have this gigantic ego that keeps you going and allows you to make the sacrifices required, in terms of your personal life and your family, for example.

A certain personality type can make that kind of sacrifice and has a big ego. At the same time, there are people like me and others who are saying, "Bring in other people, listen to other people's points of view, don't jump to conclusions, be open-minded, think about how the world's changing, and be prepared to change what you've done in the past." Boy, that's a tough message. It's difficult.

Do leaders in certain types of companies do this stuff better?
I think entrepreneurial companies tend to be more embracing of the message, almost by nature. One of the big words in strategy lately has been *pivot*: they pivot from one spot to another.

In an entrepreneurial company, that just means that you're changing your business model from something that didn't work to something that you hope is going to work. There's not that much to lose at that stage, so you do it.

For a big company to change what it's done and its portfolio of businesses into something else . . . well, there are not a lot of examples of that. The cell phone industry is an interesting example. You go from Motorola to where Nokia beat Motorola. Then you go past Nokia to Research in Motion and the BlackBerry. Then you go to the Apple iPhone, and now to Samsung.

It's an incredible story in that industry, where huge market share and huge brand name power are eclipsed by a subsequent player.

So there's a requirement that you be adaptable, open, and adjusting. Being willing to throw out what you've done in the past is not easy.

Are there different cultural responses when you travel around the world talking about Why Smart Executives Fail?

The primary tendency I see in the United States and the United Kingdom is, "Well, it's fine, you're talking to me and I buy it, but maybe you need to talk to my CEO, chairman, and executive chairman."

In other words, I get a pass-the-buck type of answer, which I never accept. Of course, there's some element of truth to that, but if you're a middle or upper-level manager, don't you have the ability to change your world, your team, your department, your office?

The answer is yes, of course you do. If you really think that it makes sense to adopt the various principles and ideas that I recommend, then you can change what you're doing in your own area.

If it's going to help you get better results, which is the whole premise, then you have a really interesting story to tell—and everyone prefers to hear good stories rather than bad stories.

And so slowly but surely the word starts to spread about this idea.

So there are cultural differences?

To be sure. When you get into Asia, with perhaps the only exception being China, there's this deference to senior leaders. There's a history of paternalistic culture, a little bit more so than we have in Western society. Also, in Hong Kong and Singapore, there are these billionaires who are in so many different businesses and have been extremely successful.

So at one level, in those environments, it tends to be tougher to get the message across; on another level, when I look at all the international translations of the book, there are more in Asia than anywhere else, and it's not just because there are more countries. They were faster, sooner, and greater in number.

Self-awareness seems to be an important theme in your book Think Again *(coauthored with Andrew Campbell and Jo Whitehead).*

Think Again is very much a book about decision making, and it gets into the micro dimensions of how people's brains work, how we process information, and, specifically, how we make decisions.

I talk about self-awareness. Working in a consulting capacity with a CEO or senior executive, the extent to which that person is self-aware is really remarkable; it comes out in a conversation so often. To me, it's really one of the most powerful leadership capabilities. That's how I label it to make it seem more practical to people, because self-awareness is a very touchy-feely type of idea once you get right down to it. But I call it a leadership capability.

The more anyone knows about how he or she thinks and behaves, his or her own biases, the less likely that person is to become a slave to that part of the brain where we just do what our gut instinct tells us to do. That can get you into a lot of trouble, so self-awareness is a big differentiator. Think again.

We suppose that self-awareness and intellectual honesty are connected with authenticity.

These are certainly ideas that overlap. For me, intellectual honesty is a little bit more outward-focused, because you're looking at the world out there, think-

ing about it, and trying to face up to it, and self-awareness is much more internally focused. But they are
related to authenticity.

CHAPTER

6

Followership

"Leadership is not defined by the exercise of power but by the capacity to increase the sense of power of those being led. The most essential work of the leader is to create more leaders," observed the early management thinker Mary Parker Follett (1868–1933).[1]

Follett was unusual. Initially, most leadership researchers focused on the leader—what were the leader's traits, behavior, or styles, for example. Some, though, were keen to explore a different aspect of leadership: the relationship between the leader and the led. After all, without followers, there can be no leadership. And, as those who chose to examine the role of the follower understood, the dynamic between the leader and the follower plays an important role in shaping leadership, for good or bad.

One of the earliest forays into the world of followers was by Abraham Zaleznik (1924–2011), a Harvard Business School professor and renowned social psychology and leadership expert who wrote "The Dynamics of Subordinacy," a 1965 *Harvard Business Review* article.[2] He approached the subject from a psychoanalytic Freudian perspective.

To Zaleznik, followers were either active or passive, submissive or controlling. Active followers wanted to engage, initiate, get involved, and take an active role in the leader-follower exchange. Passive followers, however, were happy to take a backseat, to let the leader take charge, and to let things happen. For the other dimension, controlling followers were willing to engage in a battle of wills, seeking to control their boss. Submissive followers, on the other hand, were happy to submit to the leader's will and be told what to do.

Given these dimensions, Zaleznik was able to classify followers into four types. Followers who are both active and controlling were classed as *impulsive*. These people are quite a handful to take charge of. They are spontaneous and rebellious and will try to set their own direction and lead, even when they are being led. At the same time, they can be courageous and take risks. Followers who are controlling but passive would like to take charge and dominate their leaders, but feel guilty about feeling that way and hold back. Zaleznik classified this group of followers as *compulsive*.

Active submissives are happy to submit to the leader's will, even though they find it difficult to do so. These followers were *masochistic*, according to Zaleznik. Finally, there was a group of followers who were *withdrawn*; they do little and care little about what is going on around them in the workplace. These workers, who will be familiar to most people working in organizations, do as little as they need to in order to stay in their job.

Boss Management

While having the aptitude to lead is always useful, it also pays to be able to manage your relationship with your superiors. It was this aspect of the leader-follower relationship that Harvard Business School professors John Gabarro and John Kotter later investigated.[3]

While Gabarro and Kotter admit that the phrase "managing your boss" might be seen as having slightly suspicious undertones, in fact the idea of subordinates paying attention to the quality of the relationship they have with their superiors makes good sense, both for the organization and for the individuals involved. After all, not all bosses are good leaders. Sometimes the follower needs to work at the relationship in order to get the best out of the leader-follower combination. Equally, just because someone is a great leader in terms of the way she interacts with her followers does not mean to say that she is equally effective at working productively with her own boss.

And mismanaging relationship with superiors can be costly. As Gabarro and Kotter point out, in the worst-case scenario, failing to manage your superiors properly can derail your career and tarnish your reputation.

A common mistake is to misunderstand the nature of the boss-subordinate relationship. It is a relationship of mutual dependence, with both the leader and the led depending on each other. Often, though, the subordinate is unwilling to acknowledge the extent of his dependence on his boss. This is shortsighted, especially when the subordinate is probably relying on his boss to connect him with other parts of the organization and to secure resources for him. The subordinate tends to expect his boss to know instinctively what help and support he needs in order to get his job done.

At the same time, subordinates often fail to appreciate just how dependent their leader is on them. Leaders are people with feelings (for the most part), and they are affected by the actions of their followers on both a professional and a personal level. If the followers underperform, it reflects poorly on the leader and may have an adverse impact on the leader's career. Leaders depend on their followers to be honest, dependable, open, and cooperative.

As a result, say Gabarro and Kotter, both people in the leader-follower relationship need to "have a good understanding of the other person and yourself, especially regarding strengths, weaknesses, work styles, and needs."[4] And then they need to "use this information to develop and manage a healthy working relationship—one that is compatible with both people's work styles and assets, is characterized by mutual expectations, and meets the most critical needs of the other person."

Of course, it can be difficult to tap into your boss's psyche. Who hasn't at one point or another wondered what his or her boss was really thinking, or misunderstood the boss completely? But those who really want a productive relationship with their boss need to approach the task of discovering what really makes the boss tick with a thorough determination.

At the very least, say Gabarro and Kotter, followers need to appreciate their boss's goals and pressures, strengths and weaknesses. Paying attention to the leader's behavior should be an ongoing process, enabling the follower to anticipate any changes from the norm.

Understanding yourself is easier in some respects. Access is easier. And hopefully it should not be too difficult to determine your strengths, weaknesses, objectives, goals, and work styles. The challenge is doing something about them, if needed. In terms of interacting with the boss, there is a range of reactions. At the two extremes lie counterdependent behavior and overdependent behavior.

Individuals who tend to be counterdependent resent the boss's authority over them and have a tendency to argue and rebel. They may object to being constrained, may struggle and fight just for the sake of doing so, and may see the boss as an enemy to be tolerated or even defeated. With an authoritarian boss, this relationship can get very messy and difficult.

In contrast, people who tend to be overdependent are servile and acquiescent in the extreme. They are compliant and quiet even when they know that their boss is making poor decisions, and they will not speak up even if debate and discussion are required. Overdependent executives tend "to see the boss as if he or she were an all-wise parent who should know best, should take responsibility for their careers, train them in all they need to know, and protect them from overly ambitious peers."[5]

Neither extreme of interaction is healthy or productive. And although these behaviors may be deeply ingrained in people and hard to alter, an awareness of any tendency to behave in such a way is very useful in dealing with them.

Armed with an insight into the inner workings of your own and your boss's mind, it is possible to start developing and maintaining a mutually beneficial working relationship. So, for example, the executive may need to accommodate elements of his or her boss's working style. Does the leader prefer to receive written briefings or to have a chat? Does she like to get involved with decisions as they arise, or is she happy to delegate and be kept informed on a need-to-know basis? How much information does the leader need about what his subordinate is up to?

It is wise to communicate and manage expectations effectively, erring on the side of passing on too much information rather than too little, for example. Add to this dependability, honesty, and an awareness that the boss's time is precious and should not be wasted, and the leader-follower relationship should benefit.

Follow Up

"In searching so zealously for better leaders we tend to lose sight of the people these leaders will lead. . . . Organizations stand or fall partly on the basis of how well their leaders lead, but partly also on the basis of how well their followers follow," Robert Kelley noted in a 1988 article.[6]

Given that the majority of people spend more time following than they do leading, Kelley felt that followers and the act of followership deserved some attention. What was the difference between a good and a bad follower? "What distinguishes an effective from an ineffective follower," said Kelley, "is enthusiastic, intelligent, and self-reliant participation—without star billing—in the pursuit of an organizational goal."[7]

It is easier to understand why a disaffected employee might make a poor follower, but why is there often a difference in the quality of followership among people who are equally committed to the organization? Kelley decided to look at the behaviors that lead to effective and noneffective following. He found that there were two different behavioral dimensions that accounted for the difference between effective and noneffective followership, and this led him to construct a model of followership patterns of behavior.[8]

The two dimensions focus on the way followers think and the way they act. Do the followers think for themselves, or do they expect the leader to do the thinking for them? And are they actively engaged in the relationship, bringing a positive energy to their work, or are they passive and giving off negative vibes?

Kelley constructed a two-by-two matrix, with a circle in the center that encompassed all four quadrants. At the top was independent, critical thinking, and at the bottom was dependent, uncritical thinking. At the right side of the matrix was active involvement, and at the left side was passive involvement.

Based on this model, there are five categories of followership. *Sheep* are in the lower left quadrant. Passive and uncritical, they expect their boss to think for them and motivate them. When they are given a task, they complete it, then they stop. They take no initiative and no responsibility. Although they are malleable and noncontentious, the sheep are still hard for leaders to work with, as they need to be given tasks and looked after.

In the bottom right corner, uncritical but active, are the *yes-people*. The yes-people get on with the task and get things done. But when they have finished, they always come back to the boss to see what needs doing next. They are deeply enterprising, but servile. Bosses who lack confidence tend to like yes-people, as they do not cause trouble, but are still industrious.

Up in the top left quadrant are the *alienated*. Although they are quite capable of thinking for themselves, they tend to be cynical and are likely to bring a negative energy and outlook to proceedings. They are passive in action. They can always find reasons not to take on new challenges and change. They have no plans for moving forward, and they are skeptical about what is happening at the moment. Kelley suggested that the alienated would not see their behavior this way, though. They would argue that they are mavericks, and that they are the only group of followers that is prepared to challenge the leader.

In the blob in the center, with a foot in each camp, are the *pragmatists*. Natural survivors, they like to sit on the sidelines and wait to see what happens. They are not going to be the first on board, in case they are catching the train to nowhere. But equally, they will not be the last in; no one could ever accuse of them of not getting involved eventually. The motto of the pragmatic survivors, suggested Kelley, is "better safe than sorry."

Finally, in the upper right quadrant, there are the *star* followers. These are independent critical thinkers who are also active and bring a positive energy to their relationship with the boss and to their work in the organization. These self-starters do not unquestioningly accept everything that their boss tells them. They apply critical judgment, and if they do not agree with the leader's decision, they question it, discuss it, and suggest alternative solutions. Star followers may appear to behave like leaders, but they are followers, and many people are perfectly happy with the role of highly effective follower.

As well as creating an enduring model of follower behavior, Kelley also tackled the qualities of effective followers: good at self-management; highly committed to something in addition to their own personal interests, whether that is a cause, an organization, or an idea; competent and highly skilled; and courageous and honest.

He also looked at the possible paths to followership; there are seven, each with its own motivation. *Apprentices* are followers, but they want to become leaders. *Disciples* like the leader, want to be like the leader, and want to be with the leader. *Mentees* are keen on personal development, but not necessarily with a view to leadership. *Comrades* like the experience of being with a group of people who are focusing on the same objectives. *Loyalists* are motivated to be followers by their emotional commitment to the leader. *Dreamers* have a dream—to follow. And some people just like the *lifestyle* of the follower.

As more interest in the psychological contract between leader and followers developed, thinkers began to ask what makes people prepared to follow one leader but not another. American anthropologist and psychoanalyst Michael Maccoby offered a psychological perspective on the leader-follower bond.[9]

Maccoby attributed the bond between leader and follower to transference, a concept developed by Freud to explain the attraction his patients had to him. It is the transference of experiences and emotions from past relationships (often parent-child) onto the present. So if employees believe that their bosses care about them in a pseudo parental way, then they will work harder in order to please those bosses. This situation will continue—unless, that is, the employee is able to get past this idealized version of the relationship to the reality of the situation. The employee is at work, and the boss is not his or her parent.

Five Kinds of Follower

One person who understands the power of followership is Barbara Kellerman. For Kellerman, an interest in leadership is part of the human condition. "Every part of our culture—from politics, to religion, and even personal relationships—involves some manifestation of leadership," she says. Her own interest started long before the subject became academically fashionable. As a graduate student in political science at Yale University in the early 1970s, she wrote her PhD dissertation on the German chancellor Willy Brandt.

It has proved an enduring fascination. Today, she is the James MacGregor Burns Lecturer in Public Leadership at Harvard University's John F. Kennedy School of Government and was the founding executive director of the Kennedy School's Center for Public Leadership. And while other commentators rhapsodize about leadership heroes, Kellerman provides an authoritative counterpoint in her 2008 book *Followership: How Followers Are Creating Change and Changing Leaders*.

She talked to us about why followership matters.

Have we been looking at the wrong part of the leadership equation, or have we just neglected one-half of it?
I wouldn't say we've been looking at the wrong part, although I do believe that management books have become far too leader-centric in the last 25 years or so. I would not say that it's a mistake to look at leaders. What I am claiming is that by looking only at leaders and ignoring followers entirely, we're doing a disservice not only to the way we think about leadership and management, but also to the way we practice it.

The word follower has connotations of sheeplike behavior. Is that part of the problem?

As you say, the word *follower* is often equated with being a sheep, and this is one of the several reasons that we stay away from it. The Harvard Kennedy School, for example, is all about educating leaders, and I can assure you that you won't hear a word about educating followers. Who wants to be a sheep? Everybody wants to be big and important and successful, and nobody wants to be lowly and ignored. However, as we speak, this value judgment is undergoing a profound revision.

Why is that happening now?
First of all, historically, followers have always been more important than is generally presumed. And second, because of changes in society, two of the most obvious being changes in culture and changes in technology. So, followers are more important now than ever before, and leaders are less important.

One of the problems with followership is its definition. How do you decide when someone is a follower?
Yes, it is complicated. I'll give you an example. In the United States, especially in the early years of the Bush administration, many people felt that the president of the United States, George W. Bush, was the puppet of the vice president, Dick Cheney, who was the puppeteer. So, in that sense, you can argue that Bush was a follower of Cheney.

To avoid those sorts of complexities, I define followers very clearly as those who are of lower rank. In other words, they are subordinates to their superiors in groups and organizations. And followership is simply the reaction of those of lower rank to those of higher rank. Now, followers generally go along with those of higher rank, but they by no means always do so.

Sometimes followers resist, and sometimes followers ignore their leaders. So we cannot presume, especially in this day and age, that followers will automatically follow. What we can presume is that they are those of lower rank.

So that definition is based on where someone is in the hierarchy?
It is. In an organization such as a hospital, for example, the hierarchy is generally strict. In other organizations, such as a nation, it is less so.

So not all followers are created equal?
Yes. Not only are not all followers created equal, but we have made a big mistake by lumping them all together. We spend a lot of time dissecting our leaders, but no time looking at followers. When I looked at all the different types of followers, I thought it was absolutely necessary to break them down, and absolutely necessary to break them down according to their level of activity and commitment.

So, there are five types of follower. At one end of the spectrum, there are what I call *isolates*, who are completely alienated or detached from the group or organization to which they belong. Then there are *bystanders*, who are not necessarily detached, but who choose, for whatever set of reasons, not to participate, so they stand by and do nothing. An extreme example is what happened in Nazi Germany, where many people did not agree with Hitler but stood by and did nothing. The third type of follower is the *participant*, who generally, but not always, supports the leader. Participants are generally active in the organization, but not overcommitted to it.

And the fourth type?

The fourth of the five types is the *activist*, who is gung ho in some way. These people are very active and very committed to either the organization or the leader, or they might be committed to upending the leader. Sometimes people do not support the leader but are very passive in trying to change the leadership. So, again, this is not necessarily supportive of the leader. And the last kind of follower is a group that I call the *diehards*. Those in that category, and I do mean this literally, are ready, willing, and able to die for the cause or the person in whom they believe, or whom they wish at all costs to overturn.

The last group in particular are the extreme—that could have an application in political situations and so on?

Yes, and in the military.

Coming back to a public organization, what are the implications of those different types of followers for leaders?

In this day and age, followers can make things difficult for leaders much more readily than they used to be able to do. So it is in the interest of leaders to harness the potential power of followers.

Leaders who don't pay serious attention to those who are their subordinates miss out on an enormous opportunity to lead wisely and well. You can't presume that all your subordinates are the same. You need to be able to distinguish among and between them, in order to lead appropriately for the particular audience you're trying to target. It's a bit like selling a product; you need to target your audience instead of simply trying to sell it in the same way to people who are in fact very different.

So, it's important for leaders, first, to recognize that they are vulnerable to these different sorts of followers in this day and age. And second, in a more positive sense, they need to be able to sell their product—the goals they wish to achieve—with their audience in mind.

And it is also very important for the followers. Most of us, even those who are quite near the top of the hierarchy, are followers because we have superiors. Hospitals, in particular, certainly in the United States, are traditionally very hierarchical. It is high time that followers and subordinates had a fuller understanding of what they are able to accomplish.

There are certain tactics and strategies, ways of being heard, that followers in hierarchical organizations, who historically have generally been rather timorous, can now start to understand.

We talked earlier about the extreme case of the diehard—someone who believes passionately in the cause. So are you talking potentially about a whistle-blower?

Yes, the whistle-blower is an extreme case in point. We tend to think of the whistle-blower as being a heroic figure, as being bold and daring and being ready, willing, and able to go out and trumpet the bad news, even at the sacrifice of his or her own well-being. One has to be really careful, however, because whistle-blowers do not in general fare well.

First of all, they are often not heard, so their efforts are wasted. Second, they typically pay a high price for what they do. Now, it's an important role to play; I don't diminish it. But I suggest that people undertake that role with caution, and explore other strategies before going out on their own and out on a limb. But, yes, a whistle-blower can be a diehard, as you suggest. They often pay the ultimate organizational price of being fired. Penalties of lesser degrees would be simply being marginalized, demoted, or overlooked. So, it's a high-risk strategy, and I think there are other strategies that should be followed before one decides to play the lone ranger role. That would be my advice.

What sort of strategies?

The first step is really coming to grips with an intellectual understanding of the changes that have taken place in the twenty-first century. We have ample examples in the United States. For example, I was a professor at Harvard University when the university's then president, Lawrence Summers, was upended by his faculty. You may recall that he made some controversial comments about women's abilities. Here is a good example of a leader who was undone by his followers.

So, increasingly it is not only fashionable, but actually smart to pay attention to followers. As a leader today, you have to pay greater attention to those who are your subordinates. And as far as the subordinates go, it is absolutely in their interest to have a greater understanding of the role they can potentially play. This does not necessarily have to be an adversarial role. If you think you have a good leader, it is very much in your interest to be actively supportive of that leader. If you think you have some problems with your leadership or management, then as a follower you can connect to colleagues, people who feel the same way, forming groups, forming alliances, and figuring out how some protests might work diplomatically.

So the emphasis on followership is bringing a far greater level of sophistication and understanding of the leader-follower dynamic. And this is happening the world over, including in places like China, where the leadership is being challenged in a way that was unimaginable even a decade ago. And this certainly does not exclude traditional hierarchies in the medical system, whether in the United Kingdom or the United States.

We are curious to know how followership is linked to your earlier book about bad leaders. Is good followership the antidote to bad leadership?
You're absolutely right to ask the question, because if one knows my book on bad leadership, one knows that each of the four chapters was divided into three sections, one devoted to the context, one devoted to the leader, and the third devoted to the followers. Writing that book made me understand actually as well as intellectually the importance of the follower.

There is no such thing as bad leadership without bad followership. If you have a bad leader, there must be bad followers who go along to assist and support that leader. When I raised the question in that book, I raised the question of why followers go along with these leaders. The human race has been able to attack physical disease and throw money at it, but we have been unable to attack the social disease of bad leadership. In its worst form, bad leadership has lethal implications. My answer is exactly as your question suggests: you cannot stop or even slow bad leaders unless you have good followers. It's that simple.

From Followership to Collaboration

The growing appreciation of followers is supported by fresh insights into the true nature of collaboration. In particular, Herminia Ibarra, Cora Chaired Professor of Leadership and Learning, and Professor of Organisational Behavior at INSEAD business school, sounds the death knell for command-and-control leadership with her compelling take on collaborative leadership.

Ibarra's early work focused on another of her main research interests, careers and talent management. *Working Identity: Unconventional Strategies for Reinventing Your Career* details how people reinvent themselves in the workplace.[10] More recently, her research has shifted to address leadership, and in particular networks and collaborative leadership.

With Mark Hunter, an adjunct professor and senior research fellow at the INSEAD Social Innovation Centre, Ibarra considers how leaders can build networks.[11] There are three essential types of networks to pay attention to: operational networks (those people the leader needs in order to get the day-to-day things done), personal networks (similarly minded people outside the organization that can help with personal advancement), and strategic networks (people outside the network builder's control who can help him or her achieve key organizational objectives). Ibarra also looked at the skills that leaders need if they are to leverage their networks.

Ibarra went on, with Morten Hansen, a professor of entrepreneurship at INSEAD, to look at the makeup of a collaborative leader.[12] "No company has all the resources that it needs in-house, so we have to work across boundaries. That is the essence of collaborative leadership, simply mobilizing and inspiring people to get great results working across boundaries," says Ibarra.[13] "What kind of leadership allows organizations to identify interesting collaborative opportunities, to bring the best talents to those opportunities, and then to lead the process so that it gets to an effective result."[14]

Ibarra identifies several areas that leaders need to focus on if they are to become good collaborative leaders. To start with, they need to build networks that allow them to add value collaboratively through connections. They should also engage diverse talent from a broad spectrum of the periphery. "That periphery could be other geographies, other nationalities, generational, bringing other people into the discussion, gender diversity, it could be many things," says Ibarra.[15]

Establishing conditions that are conducive to the collaborative process comes next. That includes eradicating any politics and turf wars that might obstruct collaboration. "You have to role model that from the top, if you don't have your collaborative potential at the top it just does not happen."[16]

And lastly, says Ibarra, show a strong hand. There is no requirement for collaboration on everything. A constant need for consensus can kill collaboration. Instead, the collaborative leader knows when to step back and when to take action to keep collaboration moving forward and adding value.

And, in order to master collaborative leadership, leaders will have to disavow some commonly held views on leadership. Take situational leadership and the need for command-and-control leadership in certain situations, for example.

"This idea of situational leadership is really ingrained," says Ibarra. "People believe that when times are good, they can do all the good things: they can let go; they can collaborate infinitely. But when times are hard, it is time to close ranks; now you have to direct and control. That is not true. When times are tough, that's when we need ideas, that's when we need to reach out further. I think that is the real barrier, the sense that there is a time for each, and command and control is still the answer to tough times."[17]

Leadership 2.0

Herminia Ibarra's thoughts on collaborative leadership were echoed when we interviewed Gary Hamel. Here is Hamel's take.

What do you see as the most important thing for a leader?

Pile up all the different business books by subject area, and the books on leadership make a bigger stack than those on strategy, change, or anything else. Look inside companies, and we spend a lot of time trying to produce leaders who have a certain set of capabilities, people who are bold yet prudent, strong and yet empathetic, visionary yet practical. But the fact of the matter is, there are very few of those people out there.

So if there are not a lot of leaders like this, what should organizations do?

One of the questions we have to ask is, is the problem finding or growing these extraordinary leaders? Or is it building organizations that can thrive even when they have fairly mediocre leadership?

I think it's much more the latter. If you look at any measure, democracies have outperformed totalitarian systems over the last 100 years.

When you look at the data, the thing that strikes you is that democracies are resilient and adaptable. In a democracy, power flows up and accountability flows down. In companies, it tends to be exactly the opposite. So it's not that we shouldn't strive to improve our leadership skills and capabilities, it's just that at the end of the day, I think that the notion that we're going to invest a lot of authority over strategy and direction in a small group of people at the top who are somehow superhuman is an entirely bankrupt notion.

So there is no use just relying on great leaders to steer organizations through a difficult business environment? One of the things we know about any social system is that the more highly you concentrate power in it, the less adaptable it is. There is a long list of companies that are struggling to regain their mojo where the problem isn't the recession, the problem is a fundamental shift in the business environment. They have a business model that's out of date.

Why did that happen? Nine times out of ten, it happened because the people at the top were unwilling to write off their depreciating intellectual capital. The world was changing around them, but they hung on to out-of-date beliefs about the customer, the technology, and the business model. They still had the power and the authority, and so the organization's capacity to change was held hostage to their personal willingness to adapt and change.

If not from leaders, then where is the impetus for the kind of change that is required from organizations going to come from?

We need a lot less attention on leadership and a lot more on how do you, on a day-by-day basis, exploit the collective intelligence and energy of the whole organization. How do you aggregate that intelligence and energy in a way that reveals where we should go next, the new opportunities? But as for the idea that one or two people at the top are going to be the primary decision makers and visionaries, I think that's just unsustainable in a world that is as complex and is changing as fast as the one we have right now.

I've often found it interesting that, while a lot of CEOs will talk about the need for change and how it's so important, I know of virtually no company that has trained every employee to be an internal activist. In fact, we're almost afraid of that kind of idea. This doesn't mean an anarchist, it means an activist. In democracy, change starts with ordinary people who form a new political party or start a campaign to save the environment or whatever. Yet inside organizations, we really haven't harnessed that ability of frontline people to build a coalition, advance a point of view, and start to shape policy. They're sitting there helpless. They've been taught that strategy starts at the top.

That turns out to be a self-fulfilling prophecy. If you don't take any responsibility for strategy, you have to wait until the next leader comes in. We have to change this, or our organizations are simply going to go through continuous cycles of convulsive change after they have missed critical things that are changing in the environment.

CHAPTER

7

Where Leaders Meet the World

All the successful leaders we have encountered have a positive and optimistic view of the world. They are not unrealistic, but they simply prefer to see the glass as half-full rather than half-empty.

Positivity is much in vogue thanks to the rise of positive psychology. Now, it is increasingly being applied to leadership. Among those who are in the vanguard of positive leadership is Lee Newman of Spain's IE Business School. He suggests a new approach to leadership designed to achieve behavioral advantage—"an advantage achieved by building an organization of individuals and teams that think and perform better, at all levels."

Sustainable competitive advantage in the conventional sense is no longer attainable, argues Newman, a former tech entrepreneur and McKinsey & Co consultant. However, it is possible to obtain *behavioral advantage*. This can be done, he contends, by taking the latest research and thinking in behavioral economics and positive psychology, and applying it to improve individual and organizational performance.

According to Newman, there are three main elements of positive leadership. The first is mindware training, which helps leaders understand their decision-making thought processes and enables them to think better. The second element focuses on building up people's strengths, rather than on improving their weaknesses. Companies should, says Newman, be "identifying the strengths of their people and teams and then designing the work around them. It's a win-win: better for the well-being of employees and better for the bottom line of the organization."

The third aspect of positive leadership that the leader needs to attend to is professional fitness. Leaders must ensure that they and their followers apply their learning in their everyday work.

As Newman notes, "It is positive because it is about helping professionals who are already performing well, move *up the curve* towards extraordinary performance." Thus positive leadership is "the new way forward to help companies achieve extraordinary sustainable results in the modern workplace."[1]

Leadership at the Edge of Town

Positive leadership meshes with the career-long work of Stew Friedman, practice professor of management at the Wharton School of the University of Pennsylvania. He trained as an organizational psychologist, was founding director of the Wharton Leadership Program, and was also founding director of Wharton's Work/Life Integration Project. He is the creator of the concept of Total Leadership and the author of *Total Leadership: Be a Better Leader, Have a Richer Life.*

Leadership has become a heavy industry, but when you started out, it was barely recognized as being worthy of serious study. How did you come to look at leadership?

My dissertation research 30 years ago at the University of Michigan was about how executives in large companies are prepared and selected for their positions. That led to my work on executive development, succession planning, CEO succession, and leadership development systems. In 1991 I started the Wharton Leadership Program. That was when Wharton did a major revamping of our whole curriculum. One of the critical elements of that work was to ensure that our students—more than 800 first-year MBAs—had real-world experience working together in teams and providing feedback on leading in a team environment. We created learning teams, which at that time were innovative in an MBA curriculum.

It was really in the 1980s that leadership took off.

Of course, people have been thinking about and struggling with the issue of how you develop future leaders since Plato. This is not a new issue. But in the 1980s, it took off in the modern business world.

Although there had been an emerging literature bubbling up through the 1960s and 1970s, the watershed book was Tom Peters and Robert Waterman's *In Search of Excellence*. They were the first to shine a bright light on the whole issue of culture and leadership, and the role of leadership in organizational performance.

The whole human potential movement was another important precursor to a focus on quality of life, on taking the whole person into account and seeing leadership as something that was available to everyone—not as just an executive role in a hierarchy but as a person's capacity to contribute to some larger social mission or cause.

What's really interesting in your work is the link between work/life integration and leadership.
I have pursued the idea that the solution to the work/life dilemma is leadership and that the heart of leadership is really the whole person.

I have, I hope, demonstrated and brought to life the idea that you can advance your leadership capacity, performance, and results at work and elsewhere by bringing together the different parts of your life, integrating them in an intelligent way that works for you. Behind this is the notion that each person can emerge as more of a leader than he or she currently is, and that leadership can be learned, practiced, and developed, like any performing art or sport, even if it cannot be taught.

The work/life debate is often polarized as a gender issue. You take a very different perspective.

While it has often and unfortunately been characterized thus, the work/life dilemma is certainly not a women's issue—it's a social, human, and economic issue. What I was intentionally, and subversively, trying to accomplish with the idea of Total Leadership was to create a language that enabled men to access these principles and methods and use them to better integrate their lives, and for it to be legitimate for them to do so.

So it's about leadership, performance, and measurable results in all parts of life: work, home, community, and the private self (mind, body, and spirit)—what I call "four-way wins." That's something that a man, as well as a woman, can get excited about pursuing and, perhaps more important, can feel *comfortable* pursuing.

The genesis of many of these ideas can be traced back to your time working with Ford, starting in 1999.

Yes, that absolutely transformed my thinking about just about everything. My world completely turned around by my experience as a senior executive in that incredible company for that two-and-a-half-year period. The first thing that I would say about that experience, reflecting back now almost 15 years, is how humbled I was by the challenge of trying to get anything done in a large social system.

I came away with a profoundly different kind of respect and admiration for people who spend their adult lives leading organizations and trying to get important things done in them. It's so much harder than it looks from the outside.

You were running the company's Leadership Development Center, a 50-person, $25 million operation. How did that come about?
When Jac Nasser became CEO of Ford, he was looking to transform the culture of the company and to change the mindset of employees to focus more on the consumer and less on the manufacturing side. He wanted everyone in the company to be outward-facing, to really take in the environment, and to see themselves as leaders in all the different parts of their lives.

Interviewing for the job, I told Jac that what I was going to do here, if he were to hire me, was to make leadership development be about the whole person, and not just about business. And when he said, "Great, I love it!" that sealed the deal for me.

It's still contrary to what a lot of people think companies should be worrying about. But we have come a long way. It's amazing to reflect on how different the world is today with respect to the legitimacy and value of leadership development. It's definitely an idea that is now fully embraced. It's also heartening to see how men are now much more comfortable talking about work/life dilemmas and seeing leadership from the point of view of the whole person.

And yet people still complain that there's a shortage of leaders.

Yes, that's true. We have a long way to go in terms of how we think about the centrality of developing leadership capacity and giving people a sense of confidence and competence in creating meaningful and sustainable change in their lives—a primary goal of the Total Leadership approach. There's still so much effort and talent being wasted as a result of our not taking this issue seriously enough. But that's not to say that we haven't made a lot of progress.

What is your current research looking at?

One question I get asked a lot is this: "A whole person view of leadership sounds good in theory, Stew, but in the real world, you can't really do anything great unless you're completely and fully dedicated to it, right?" I have been asking students and others to write short biographies of people whom they admire and who exemplify the principles of Total Leadership: who have figured out for themselves what it means for them to *be real* (to act with authenticity by clarifying what matters to them), to *be whole* (to act with integrity by respecting the whole person), and to *be innovative* (to act with creativity by continually experimenting with how things get done). These are people who have achieved greatness in the world not in spite of their commitments to other parts of their lives, but *because* of how their work benefits from their investments in family, community, and the private self.

The mythology is that you have to write off the rest of your life in order to have success as a leader. Of course, you always have to make sacrifices at some point. But there are many examples of people who have drawn power, wisdom, and support from their families, from their communities, and from their emotional and spiritual lives in order to achieve great things in their professional lives by finding mutual value among the different parts of life. Indeed, this is the story I tell in my book *Great Leaders, Good Lives*.[2]

The Total Leadership message is to have a systematic and disciplined approach to focusing on what matters most to you and to the people around you, and then experimenting with ways of creating what I call four-way wins. We have identified a set of skills that bring to life the three main principles of being real, being whole, and being innovative. *Great Leaders, Good Lives* will feature six great leaders who've lived good lives and an analysis of the skills they've used to do so. It will show how anyone can practice those skills.

You are also still leading Wharton's Work/Life Integration Project.

The Work/Life Integration Project started in 1991 and had two primary missions. One was to bring together thought leaders in business, academia, and the public sector and to have them discover and share best practices in integrating the different parts of life at the individual level, the executive level, and the organization and societal level.

The other part of the project was research on the lives and careers of Wharton students and alumni. The first product of that was the 2000 book *Work and Family—Allies or Enemies?*[3] In 1992 we gathered in-depth survey data from the graduating class, and 20 years later we administered the same survey to the graduates of the class of 2012. Then we went back to the class of 1992 and asked them further questions about their lives, careers, achievements, and future aspirations. And we asked them how they deal with work/life challenges, their views on dual-career relationships, how their work has evolved, how technology has affected them, and so on.

One of the questions we asked of both classes was, do you plan to have children? In 1992, 79 percent of men and women said yes, and in 2012, 42 percent said yes. Another book, called *Baby Bust*, looks at how the past two decades have seen enormous changes in both work and family life.[4] I describe why and how things have changed, and in very different ways for men and for women. For example, the reasons why fewer men are planning to have children are not the same as the reasons why fewer women are planning to have children.

The good news is that there is a growing convergence between men and women in terms of their attitudes and values concerning both work and family life. And the ideas and methods in the Total Leadership program can help them create a new social order. That is, among the key takeaways from the Total Leadership program is that people learn to recognize that they have a lot more power and discretion to create change and to harness that power. This enables them to attend to the things that matter most to them and to make a greater contribution to the world in ways that work for them and for the people around them.

What's so exciting about this moment in history is that we're taking the idea of human liberation one step further. Earlier in my life, in the 1960s, there was an explosion of interest in liberating the human spirit. The next phase of our evolution is under way. There's so much experimentation now in terms of the ways that families live their lives, with many young people questioning what's possible and acceptable. And, of course, the advent of the digital revolution has accelerated everything. There are going to be a lot more options available to people, men and women, for how they choose to work and how they contribute.

Do you think of yourself as a leader?

I want everyone to think of him- or herself as a leader, and certainly that applies to me too. My main conception of what leaders do is that they bring people together, they mobilize people, to accomplish some valued goal. And for it to be valuable, the goal has to make things better for other people. So that's my mission through my work, and that's an idea that I'm trying my best to help cultivate wherever I go—with our students at Wharton and beyond. Each of us needs to be him- or herself in whatever sphere we're in—at work, at home, in the community, and alone with our private thoughts. We need to bring ourselves in full to all the important domains in our lives to make the world better.

There is a powerful strain of optimism in your work.
Well, I'm glad you picked that up, because to me, it is the hallmark of what leaders have to do: to convert the harsh realities of today into a hopeful path to make the world a little better. It is about looking at reality as clearly as you can, and then creatively, and in concert with other people, trying to figure out ways to improve the human condition.

CHAPTER

8

Leaders at Work

For anyone who is interested in learning more about leadership, there are plenty of resources to choose from—so many, in fact, that the biggest challenge may be knowing where to start. The leadership thinkers in this book represent some of the most respected thinkers in their field, and any leadership reading list would feature many of their books and articles.

But what happens when the leader, or would-be leader, has pored over countless seminal works on the subject, when the bookshelves are sagging under the weight of leadership classics, when the Kindle is almost worn out? After making copious notes, underlining passages, drawing mind maps, and writing crib cards, the leader actually has to go to work and do some leading.

Most publications on leadership, even the most theoretical, contain some practical pointers for leaders, or indeed followers. However, some leadership thinkers are particularly focused on leadership in practice—not so much on the traits, characteristics, and attributes, perhaps, but certainly on the functional, practical side of leadership.

Leadership in Action

Take John Adair, a senior lecturer at Sandhurst, the British Royal Military Academy. The military is the classic example of the benefits of great leadership in practice. Great leaders conquer nations. Poor leaders get their troops killed, and possibly themselves as well. Understandably, Adair was focused on the practical application of leadership theory in the field.

Adair felt that the leadership training he had received in the army could be improved. "The kind of instruction I was given, as a second lieutenant in my National Service days (training to be one), was a list of 32 essential qualities of a leader," he later observed.

To replace the qualities or traits approach, Adair developed a functional approach to leadership. He identified the key leadership functions as planning, initiating, controlling, supporting, informing, and evaluating.

He is best known for the Action Centered Leadership model. In Adair's view, leadership was tempered through action—being placed in situations where leaders could experience leadership for themselves. His model was one of three overlapping areas of leadership responsibility: team, task, and individual. The leader, he said, had a responsibility to help a group to achieve its task, to build it as a team, and to develop and motivate the individual members.

According to Adair's model, a significant part of the leader's role is maintaining balance among the three elements. If the team becomes too dominant, it will degenerate into a committee. Concentrate too much on the task, and the leader ends up as a dictator. Fail to focus on the individual, and anarchy beckons.

During the 1970s, Adair took his model from the lecture rooms of the officer class to the boardrooms of industry. Adair's conception of three overlapping areas of task, team, and individual was condensed into a Venn diagram of three interlocked circles. The logo was printed on laminated cards and handed to countless supervisors and managers.

In the business context, Action Centered Leadership was all about transforming managers from administrators into leaders. His functional approach to leadership was widely applied in business. This was partly because of his strong support for leadership training in companies and his involvement with the Industrial Society.

Adair believed that the skills of leadership were practical and could be learned by almost anyone. He was clearly ahead of his time in anticipating future leadership trends. "To compete and grow in global marketplaces, companies must concentrate on being creative and innovative, and to achieve this they will need people-centered leaders, not old-style macho managers. But too many managers will see themselves as controllers, allocators, or accountants."

Tipping Point Leadership

While Adair drew on his experiences of military leadership to create more effective leaders in practice, W. Chan Kim and Renée Mauborgne, professors at the international business school INSEAD, looked at leadership in a different public service, where leadership is equally critical.

In their article in the April 2003 issue of the *Harvard Business Review* entitled "Tipping Point Leadership," Kim and Mauborgne point to the work of New York City police chief William Bratton as an example of what they termed "tipping point leadership."

There was a crime surge in New York during the mid-1990s. Low pay, dangerous working conditions, and long hours had created a disillusioned and poorly motivated police force. The New York Police Department (NYPD) lacked sufficient resources, and organizational politics were rife.

According to Kim and Mauborgne, Bratton's leadership was built around four elements: the cognitive (communicating and ensuring that managers were in touch with the problems), politics (keeping internal foes quiet and isolating external ones), resources (initially concentrating on trouble areas), and motivation (matching messages to various levels within the organization).

Bratton employed a range of tactics to implement his strategy and address the four obstacles. He dealt with cognitive obstacles by forcing senior management to confront problems face-to-face. For example, the statistics suggested that the subway was a safe way to travel, yet anecdotal evidence from the people who used it said otherwise. Bratton made his police chiefs and middle management ride the subway regularly so that they could see the reality—gangs, aggressive begging, fare dodging, and crime—firsthand.

There will always be powerful vested interests arrayed against the tipping point leader who is trying to implement change. In the case of organizational politics, three factors have a disproportional effect: angels (those who have the most to gain from the strategic shift), devils (those who have the most to lose), and the consigliere (a highly respected insider who can guide the tipping point leader through the political minefield).

For tipping point leaders, the plan of action should be, first, find a respected consigliere. Second, identify and attempt to isolate devils by building a broad coalition of support and anticipating and devising ripostes to likely objections.

Kim and Mauborgne suggest that tipping point leaders focus on three factors that have a disproportionate influence on motivation: kingpins, fishbowl management, and atomization.

Start with the kingpins: key influencers in the organization. Bratton focused on the 76 precinct heads at the NYPD. Through them, he knew that he could reach between two and four hundred senior police officers, and 35,000 police on the front line.

Then, through a process of transparency, inclusion, and fair process, shine a light on the kingpins' actions, both good and not so good. This almost instantly creates a high-performance culture, as kingpins do not wish to be seen in a poor light.

Finally, a tipping point leader tries to make the task more manageable. Therefore, Bratton looked at the task as a street-by-street, block-by-block, precinct-by-precinct challenge, making the prospect of taming crime in a city the size of New York less intimidating and more achievable.

In tackling the resource challenge, Bratton focused the resources that were available on hot spots, meaning that these activities needed fewer resources, but provided an opportunity for large performance gains. For example, subway crime was concentrated in a few lines and stations, yet when Bratton began, most lines and stations had an equal police presence. The solution: transfer more police to the hot spots.

At the same time, deal with those activities that consume a lot of resources, but make comparatively little contribution to performance. Processing criminals in court, even for the pettiest of crimes, took 16 hours, with much of that time being spent on the transfer of the suspect from the crime scene to court. Bratton introduced "bust buses" that took the processing to the crime scene.

Tipping point leadership works. In just two years, Bratton cut felonies by 39 percent, murders by 50 percent, and theft by 35 percent. His track record also includes successful stints at the New York Transit Police, Boston Metropolitan Police, Massachusetts Bay Transit Authority, Boston Police District Four, and Los Angeles Police Department. In all these organizations, he brought about significant change.

Making the Transition

For more than 20 years, Linda A. Hill, the Wallace Brett Donham Professor of Business Administration at Harvard Business School, has studied people who are moving into leadership positions, particularly high-potential talent moving into management for the first time. Her early research followed a small number of managers over the course of their first year in a leadership position. The results formed part of her 1992 book *Becoming a Manager*.

Over the years, Hill observed that the challenge of that first leadership position was becoming ever more difficult. One of the reasons people that find the transition difficult, says Hill, is because of a number of misconceptions that they have about the role.[1] New leaders assume that they will have a lot of authority and power and will be able to exercise them freely. In fact, they often find that they are constrained by all the connections and relationships that they need to deal with in order to do their job as leader. The sooner they learn to manage those networked relationships, the sooner they will be able to come to grips with their new role.

Another myth is that authority flows naturally from the leadership position. Direct reports do what they are told because the leader told them to do it. However, new leaders soon discover that this is not the case. Instead, says Hill, the new leader needs to demonstrate character (that is, the intention to do the right thing) and competence in his or her new role; this does not have to be technical prowess, but might just as easily be a willingness to ask questions and to listen. In addition, new leaders need to show that they can use the influence that comes from their connections with the organization.

Showing the team who's boss as soon as they arrive in their new position is a common mistake that new leaders make. Compliance and control exercised through formal power will not prove effective for long. It's better to share power and influence than to give orders, says Hill. Equally, managing one-on-one is useful, but new leaders need to create a team atmosphere and build a collaborative, team-driven context for individuals to operate within.

Finally, new leaders need to create the conditions for their team's success. This means sticking up for their team and using their power and influence to further the interests of the group.

In "Are You a Good Boss—or a Great One?," Hill and Kent Lineback return to some of the same themes, making the observation that a lot of bosses fail to fulfill their full potential because they neglect to continue developing their talents.[2] They fail to ask the questions "How good am I?" and "Do I need to be better?" The authors suggest that not enough bosses really know what they need to do in order to be truly effective, or where they want to be in the future. Hill and Lineback suggest an approach that will help leaders fulfill their potential. They call it the three imperatives: manage yourself, manage a network, and manage a team.

Leaders need to influence others if they are to succeed. At the same time, followers will be observing their boss at work and making judgments about whether or not they are willing to let the leader influence them. The followers must trust their boss in order to be influenced. If trust is the result of competence and character, leaders must manage themselves in ways that display their competence and character and thus inspire trust.

Effective leaders manage their network well. Rather than recoiling from organizational politics, they embrace it, knowing that they need to make the right contacts in the organization if they are to exert influence in a productive way. Building an informal network throughout the organization and engaging in organizational politics is the best way to ensure that they have the resources and the power to get things done. Not only do effective leaders build and maintain these connections, but they also make sure that they do so on several levels—including their own boss in their network, for example.

When you are leading a team, it can be tempting to deal with team members individually rather than collectively. Time is precious. Everyone is working hard. Online virtual team meetings are not always that effective. Yet people like to be part of a team, to share common goals and feel that sense of collective purpose. Even if it is not the easiest option, an effective leader manages the team as a team and not as a group of individuals. Everyone needs to be included. Certainly individuals will sometimes need to be dealt with individually, but those interactions can always be freehand in a team context.

Finally, the effective leader needs to keep tabs on how he or she is doing with the three imperatives. Fortunately, Hill and Lineback provide a checklist questionnaire to help leaders keep score.

Future–Engage–Deliver

Steve Radcliffe is a leadership and development consultant who has worked alongside a number of CEOs of major organizations, from Unilever to the United Kingdom's Civil Service. He is the author of *Leadership: Plain and Simple*.[3]

Radcliffe's mission is to persuade people that leadership does not have to be difficult. Most people can learn to be more effective leaders, whether they are the CEO of a multinational corporation or have just started work.

> It absolutely doesn't matter where you are in an organization. You can be in your first job, you can have no direct reports. You can have a team or run a department. You can head an organization. And you can

work in a school, charity or global business. It really doesn't matter because I've seen inspiring leadership from people in all these positions and I've realized that the fundamentals of leadership are the same for any situation.[4]

Whatever the position, there are three essential ingredients to focus on, says Radcliffe: Future–Engage–Deliver.

Leading has to start with the future and where the leader wants to get to. Only by having a strong sense of where they need to be in the future will leaders be able to persuade others to commit to that future too. The more passionately a leader cares about that future, the greater the positive impact on the followers.

Next, leaders have to engage, says Radcliffe. As he points out, this is not "communicating to," "presenting at," or "telling." This is engaging people both in the vision of the future and with the leader. The qualities required to achieve this include "integrity, openness and consistency," Radcliffe notes. Finally, the leaders need to deliver, or, more to the point, to help the team to help the leader deliver.

Improving in these areas means building and flexing leadership muscles. We all have them; it is just a question of exercising them effectively.

Mojo Location

If anyone knows leaders, it must be Marshall Goldsmith; he has met enough of them. As one of the world's best-known executive coaches (the *Wall Street Journal* ranked him among the top

10 executive educators), Goldsmith has racked up an impressive seven million air miles from his California base and coached more than 70 major CEOs. His books include *Coaching for Leadership*, *The Leader of the Future*, and *What Got You Here Won't Get You There*.

To what extent is being a leader about putting on a performance?

That is a very good question. The example I use with the executives that I work with is a Broadway or a West End play. People in a show do not say, "Oh, my foot hurts; I don't feel too good today; I'm in a bad mood." Why? Because it is showtime.

I tell the executives, "The kid on the stage is making 2 percent of what you're making. If the kid can go out there, night after night after night, and be a professional, then so can you."

But how does that tie in with authenticity?

You use the word *authentic*. But this isn't being a phony; this is being a professional. If you're the CEO of a multibillion-dollar corporation, and you're in a meeting, everyone in that room is looking at your face. They're listening to every word you say, and it matters to them.

Now, CEOs are human. Sometimes you're in a meeting, someone's making a presentation, it's boring, you already know what the person's going to say, and you've got to go to the bathroom.

It doesn't matter. They're all looking at your face, and if you don't look interested and caring and motivated, you demoralize people. That's what being a professional is.

What about your book Mojo?

Well it is very different from the previous book, *What Got You Here Won't Get You There*. That book is about interpersonal relationships. *Mojo* is much more intrapersonal. It's on the inside, and in the book *Mojo*, I focus on achieving happiness and meaning in our lives, doing what makes us happy, and doing what is meaningful for us.

I always ask the question, what are the number one characteristics of successful people? One of the key answers is that successful people are engaged in behavior that does two things at once. One, it makes them happy. And two, it's meaningful for them.

Managing the succession process is an important role for leaders. You wrote a book about that—how do leaders do succession well?

I talk about three variables that the person who is getting ready to leave needs to work on. One is, of course, that you still have to run your company or your business, whatever it happens to be.

Two, you need to develop your successor, of course.

Three, which is seldom discussed, you need to find something else to do.

*So it is a very practical look at this aspect of
leadership?*

What I like about this succession book is that it talks
about the reality of succession. Rather than pretending that this is a process in which everybody talks
about long-term shareholder value, it covers the
human dimension. What does succession feel like?
What does it feel like to let go? What does it feel like
to give up what you're doing?

Of course, the reality is that it's hard. It is very,
very hard.

Take a relay race, for example. It's tough. If
you're ahead in the relay race, everybody's cheering,
keep going, don't stop. And if you're behind, then
you don't want to stop. You feel like, I've got to catch
up, I've got to catch up.

So either way, it is hard to let go. In the book
Succession: Are You Ready?, I talk about the dynamics
of letting go, and why it's important. I also talk about
how hard it is. I've done three sessions, with 11 CEOs
in each session, talking about letting go. I can tell you,
it's easy in theory, but not easy in practice.

*It was Peter Drucker who said that we spend too much
time telling leaders what they should do, and not
enough time telling them what they should not do.
Do you agree with that?*

Totally. Peter Drucker said that we spend a lot of time
helping leaders learn what to do, and not enough time
helping leaders learn what to stop.

That quote was actually the inspiration for my book *What Got You Here Won't Get You There*. A lot of that book is about teaching successful leaders what to stop.

A lot of times, when we coach people, what we tell them isn't deep or profound, it's simple: quit doing this. And if people learn to quit doing things, they get better. For example, if you're stubborn and opinionated, I teach people, don't start sentences with *no*, *but*, or *however*. I fine my clients $20 every time they do it.

So I'm going over one client's 360-degree feedback, and he says, "But Marshall," and I say, "It's free this time, but if I talk to you again and you start a sentence with *no*, *but*, or *however*, I'm going to fine you $20." He says, "But Marshall": $20. "No": $40. "No, no, no": $60, $80, $100. He lost $420 in an hour and a half. At the end of an hour and a half, he said to me, "Thank you. I had no idea. I did that 21 times with you throwing it in my face. How many times would I have done it if you had not been throwing it in my face? 50? 100? No wonder people think I'm stubborn and opinionated."

You mentioned the words thank you. *How important are those words in leadership?*
Very important. And they don't become less important the higher up you go. They become more important.

Every decision is made by the person who has the power to make that decision, not the smartest person or the best person or the right person. The higher up you go, the more you are that person. You get to win. You get to win all the time. It is very hard for leaders to let go of this desire to prove that they're smart, or right, or good, and to thank other people, to recognize the contributions of others.

But let the other person be smart. Let the other person be right. Let the other person win. If you're the CEO, you get to win anyway. You don't need to take credit; you need to give credit.

To me, the more you can let other people take ownership of ideas, thank them for their contributions, and make them feel good about what they're doing for the organization, the better off everyone is.

We have been talking about leadership, but tell us a little bit about your coaching methods.
My job is to help leaders who are already successful achieve positive, lasting change in behavior for themselves and the people on their teams. So what I do is very specific and focused. It's about not fixing problems, but about helping people who are already very successful, great people try to get better.

My coaching method is unique. I don't get paid if my clients don't get better, and whether they get better is not judged by me or by my clients. It's judged by everyone around my clients.

So how often do you not get paid? Has it ever happened?

It's happened. Not a lot; 10 or 15 percent of the time I don't get paid for a variety of different reasons. But the way my coaching process works is very straight-forward.

The person who is receiving the coaching has to get confidential feedback on how everyone sees him. He is going to find out what he's doing well and what he needs to improve. The people around him venture suggestions. Then he and I sit down, possibly with his boss, and talk. We have to reach an agreement. He's going to have to get the feedback, talk to people, follow up on a regular, disciplined basis, and apologize for previous sins.

And my contract is simple: you get better. If the right behavior is judged by the right people, it's worth this money. And I tell the people, if it's not worth the money, don't do it. If it is worth the money, you can't lose. You get better, I get paid. You don't get better, it's free.

And what about the FeedForward element? Tell us a little bit about that.

Well I'm a Buddhist, a philosophical Buddhist. FeedForward is a very Buddhist concept. In FeedForward, I teach people, don't ask for feedback about the past; ask for ideas about the future.

And I teach my clients to shut up, listen, take notes, and say thank you. No matter what the person says, just say thank you. Don't promise to do everything that people suggest. Leadership is not a popularity contest. My clients just listen and think about what people say, write it down, and then they do what they can.

It's focused on a future that you can change, not a past that you can't change. It doesn't involve putting anyone down or insulting anyone. No judging is allowed, so it's very positive and upbeat. People like it, and you get about 80 percent of the benefit of feedback. You miss all the cost of the anger, the putting people down, and the defensiveness. I love the FeedForward idea; it's the essence of my coaching process.

And what makes a good executive coach like yourself? What are the qualities? And what have you learned from what you do?

You know, I think the biggest quality is letting go of your own ego. If I had to look at my failures in life as a coach, the number one failure would be me.

The clients I coached that improved are the clients that I spent the least amount of time with. The clients I coached that didn't improve at all, so I didn't get paid, are those that I spent the most amount of time with.

I said to one of my clients, "What should I learn from you?" He said, "Marshall, a couple of things. The first thing you need to learn as a coach is that your number one job is client selection. If you have the right clients, your coaching process will always work. If you have the wrong clients, your coaching process will never work." And he said, "My job isn't that different. I have to manage great people. It doesn't matter how good I am as a leader. If I have the wrong people, I'm not going to be successful."

He then said, "The second learning point is, don't make the coaching process about you. This wasn't about you and your ego; it was about me and my team. Don't get lost in yourself." He added, "My job is the same. As a great achiever, it's all about me. As a great leader, it's all about them."

The hard lesson for a coach as a great coach is that it's not about you, it's about your clients. And the one thing I've learned as a coach, a very hard lesson, is that it's not about me.

You have a process with your peer coach where you go through a series of questions. Can you reveal what some of those questions are?

Well, let me describe some of the specific questions. And the way the process works, by the way, is that my questions are intended for me. The idea of the question process is that you write your own questions.

I'll share some of mine, though, just in case others might be interested. The first question every day is: "On a 1 to 10 scale, how happy were you yesterday?" I don't have to work. I live in a nice place. I have nice friends and family and wonderful clients.

If I'm not happy, whose problem is that? Look in a mirror.

"On a 1 to 10 scale, how meaningful was yesterday?" Did I do something that mattered, something that was important, or did I just waste time?

"How many times did you try to prove you were right when it wasn't worth it?" I hate to say this, but I've almost never in my life gotten zero. It is hard not to do this.

"How many angry or destructive comments did you make about other people?" "Did you say or do something nice for your wife, your son, or your daughter?"

"How many minutes did you write?" I don't know. I've written 28 or 29 books. They don't write themselves. You actually have to do the work.

"Are you updated on your clients?" "How much do you weigh?" "How many alcoholic drinks did you have?" They're just basic questions about life, and I find that this keeps me focused.

Someone once asked me, "Why do you need to do this? Don't you know the theory about how to change behavior?"

I wrote the theory. That's why I do it.

Cracking the Leadership Code

As a coda for leaders, *The Leadership Code: Five Rules to Lead By* is persuasive. Coauthor Kate Sweetman is a visiting scholar at the

Legatum Center for Development and Entrepreneurship at the Massachusetts Institute of Technology (MIT), where she works with gifted young entrepreneurs from emerging and developing countries.

What can followers do to make sure that they get good leaders?

The fact is, organizations need a lot of leaders, but they are probably going to have more followers than leaders.

The five elements of the leadership code are actually not a bad list to tick through if you're thinking about whether a place is somewhere you might like to work, from a leadership perspective.

What kinds of questions should you ask yourself?

For example, begin by asking whether you think that the people who are at the decision-making level really have a good sense of where they are going. Do they have a vision, a mission, a strategy, or whatever they are calling it, about how they are going to translate the organization into the future?

Second, do they appear to know how to execute on that strategy? Do things seem to work smoothly; do their products get to market; do things really happen?

Third, do they really know how to connect to their own people? Often, particularly in these difficult times, organizations are so focused on execution that they forget that there are human beings behind the organization. What is the feel of the place, the pulse? Do people seem to be excited to come to work and happy to be there, and do they feel like there is a future for them, or is the tone around the place more that it is not really a place where you are going to be able to move forward?

Is there anything else?

Well, when you get in to meet the individual you are going to work for, what is your sense of him or her as a person? Is this really somebody whom you can rely on and trust, who you think is going to be looking out for you as well as for his or her own interests?

So, there is a sort of complex assessment that you need to make, but I think it is a worthwhile one.

What was the idea that you set out with?

The reason we wrote *The Leadership Code* was not so much to come up with a new model of leadership or a revolutionary new way to think about it; it was really more about trying to make some order of the very confusing universe of leadership.

I have been working in leadership for 20 years. I have been in many organizations, and it is obvious that organizations, and different parts of organizations, choose different elements of leadership to emphasize. It might be emotional intelligence, or adaptive leadership, or situational leadership, for example.

But what does it all really add up to for these organizations? What we have tried to do is to look at what all leadership has in common and how these different ideas really fit in, so that when you are choosing to become a leader or to develop leadership in an organization, you know that you have thought about it in a thorough and balanced way.

Are there common elements to good leadership?

Absolutely. On the face of it, you would think that Mother Teresa had very little in common with Winston Churchill, for example. But, in fact, when you consider them more closely and you look at good leaders who could really build organizations that lasted, in all sorts of endeavors, what you find is that 60 to 70 percent of what they do is actually the same.

If the five rules account for two-thirds of what makes a leader effective, what else is important?

The other components really depend on the situation—on whether you are trying to run a pharmaceutical company in a certain way or whether you are trying to marshal an army, for example. That's why a leader who is successful in one endeavor sometimes is not so successful in another.

Can you elaborate on the individual elements of the leadership code?

The five rules of the leadership code really have to do with the long and the short term, and with the business and the people.

So, if you think about a classic four-square consulting matrix, in the upper right-hand corner is someone who thinks about the long term and is really focused on the business, so that is the *strategist*. Thus, the strategist piece of leadership is really about understanding the larger picture, scanning the environment, and talking to external stakeholders— in particular, customers. It is also about really understanding, from the inside of the organization, what you know about the world and therefore where you can go with the organization.

Another important piece of strategy that leaders sometimes forget about is what we call *strategic traction*. As you formulate the strategy, remember that there's an organization that needs to execute on it. So while part of the strategy formulation is possibly about stretch, it also has to include the organization's capability to deliver against that.

What comes next?

The second part of the leadership code we call the *executor*. The executor is focused on the business, but is able to act in the short term. It is what some people might call management, but it is the part of leadership that is really about making it happen.

So there is a change plan in place and a methodology for going about it, and the leader knows how the decisions are going to be made and who's going to do it. This is where you work through a lot of those team issues to make sure that everyone is put together in a way that will move the plan forward, tied to the strategy.

How about the third part?

The box in the bottom left is where the people element meets the short term. So, if we are leaders, we have got to be able to *communicate* with the people who are surrounding us right now, letting them know exactly what it is required.

At times when people are living through a lot of difficulties and uncertainties, for example, it is almost impossible to overcommunicate. Often we see in organizations that when the boss is off planning some exotic strategy or coming up with a method for the organization to go forward, the employees really need to have someone talk with them because they need to know what's going on.

This dimension is also about connecting with your people, understanding their motivation, and managing the available talent.

And the fourth dimension?

This is the part that most organizations miss the most: *human capital development.* It is where strategy concerning the business meets people in the long term. So, what human capital development is really about is, given where the leader thinks the organization is heading, how is it going to be organized? Regionally, where will it be located and operating? What are the key jobs going to be? Do we have a sense of who is going to be able to fill those kinds of jobs? And so on.

Those are the four external dimensions of a leader, then, plus there is also a fifth element of understanding yourself as a leader. Is that right?

Yes. This dimension is about the source of the leader. Think of it as the personal proficiency dimension, really. It is an area that there has been a lot of work on, and where there has been a lot of coverage in the press and in the media. So, for example, it is the dimension where you would be including elements such as emotional intelligence and authentic leadership.

But what we call *personal proficiency* is basically the things that emerge from you as a person that are able to help you to do these other jobs well: being a strategist, being an executor, dealing with people, and figuring out the map of the future and the people map of the future. So, when you think about personal proficiency, it really has to be about leaders understanding what it is that they want to accomplish.

Simple, Really

In the final analysis, leadership is simple. But leading day after day in a complex organization is hugely difficult. Chris Zook of Bain & Company talks about a concept he calls "commander's intent." This is how he explained it to us:

Over time, actually tracing back to the 1700s and 1800s even, through naval combat and Napoleonic wars, the phrase *commander's intent* emerged. It came from a situation where a number of people, such as Admiral Nelson and others, found it very powerful to be able to have a very simple statement that every one of the commanders knew and understood.

It was a statement of the strategy and some of the nonnegotiable principles of behavior, because unexpected elements always emerge during combat, and the more decisions that you can push down to the front line, the better.

Admiral Nelson is believed to have been so successful, winning so many naval engagements, in part because he and his band of brothers, the other captains, had a relatively clear set of principles of behavior. This meant that his captains, even under unexpected conditions, even when they were over the horizon and unable to see Nelson, for example, could almost anticipate how the others would behave.

In business, the analogy is the nonnegotiable principles of the business. Many of the most successful and enduring businesses are those that have actually been able to push decisions closer to the front line, with fewer layers in the middle. This is because the commander's intent, the essence of what the business was trying to do, and the key nonnegotiable principles were so well understood.

Take the example of Vanguard, the biggest investment company in the world. Vanguard has obsessively focused on the small investor, rather than the big investor, which is the more lucrative segment that most companies focus on. It has focused on being low cost through its mutual structure and expenses, and on index funds because it believes, as one of its nonnegotiable principles, that the small investor cannot beat the market consistently without inside information. These types of principles and statements are as clearly stated by the CEO as they are by the person on the phone speaking to the customer. That allows much more action, more learning, and more decisions that can be pushed down to the front line, and also for insights to be fed back in a more orderly way. In the final analysis, leadership is a multifaceted balancing act. It involves principles. It requires action. It demands learning. And it is driven by context as much as personal energy and ambition. It is dauntingly human.

Notes

Chapter 1

1. Bennis, W., and Nanus, B., *On Becoming a Leader*, Reading, MA: Addison-Wesley Publishing Company, 1989.
2. French, J. P. R., Jr., and Raven, B., "The Bases of Social Power," in *Group Dynamics*, ed. D. Cartwright and A. Zander, New York: Harper and Row, 1960.
3. Blake, R., and Mouton, J., *The Managerial Grid: The Key to Leadership Excellence*, Houston: Gulf Publishing Co, 1964.
4. Adair, J. E., *Action-Centred Leadership*, London: McGraw-Hill, 1973.
5. Hersey, P., and Blanchard, K. H., *Management of Organizational Behavior: Utilizing Human Resources*, 3rd ed., Englewood Cliffs, NJ: Prentice Hall, 1977.
6. Fiedler, F. E., "A Contingency Model of Leadership Effectiveness," in *Advances in Experimental Social Psychology*, ed. L. Berkowitz, Academic Press, 1964; and

Fiedler, F. E., *A Theory of Leadership Effectiveness*, New York: McGraw-Hill, 1967.

7. Burns, J. M., *Leadership*, Harper & Row, 1978.

8. Bass, B. M., "From Transactional to Transformational Leadership: Learning to Share the Vision," *Organizational Dynamics*, Winter 1990.

7. Gladwell, Malcolm, *The Tipping Point: How Little Things Can Make a Big Difference*, Boston: Little, Brown, 2000.

8. Kim, W. C., and Mauborgne, R., "Tipping Point Leadership," *Harvard Business Review*, April 2003.

9. Goleman, Daniel, Boyatzis, Richard, and McKee, Annie, "Primal Leadership: The Hidden Driver of Great Performance," *Harvard Business Review*, December 2001.

10. Klein, K., Ziegert, J., Knight, A., and Xiao, Y., "A Leadership System for Emergency Action Teams: Rigid Hierarchy and Dynamic Flexibility," *Academy of Management Journal*, July 2004.

11. Gratton, Lynda, *The Democratic Enterprise: Liberating Your Business with Freedom, Flexibility, and Commitment*, London: Financial Times/Prentice Hall, 2003.

12. Collins, James C., *Good to Great: Why Some Companies Make the Leap . . . and Others Don't*, New York: HarperBusiness, 2001.

13. Maccoby, Michael, "Narcissistic Leaders: The Incredible Pros, the Inevitable Cons," *Harvard Business Review*, January 2004.

14. Kotter, John, and Gabarro, John, "Managing Your Boss," *Harvard Business Review*, January 1980.

15. Kelley, R. E., "In Praise of Followers," *Harvard Business Review*, November 1988.

16. Kellerman, Barbara, *Followership: How Followers Are Creating Change and Changing Leaders*, Boston: Harvard Business School Press, 2008.

Chapter 2

1. Bennis, Warren G., and Thomas, Robert J., "Crucibles of Leadership," *Harvard Business Review*, September 2002.
2. Ibid.
3. All quotations are from author interviews unless otherwise noted.
4. Bennis, Warren G., and Slater, Philip E., *The Temporary Society*, New York: Harper and Row, 1968.
5. Bennis, Warren G., *An Invented Life: Reflections on Leadership and Change*, Reading, MA: Addison-Wesley, 1993.
6. Bennis, Warren G., and Nanus, Burt, *Leaders: Strategies for Taking Charge*, New York: Harper and Row, 1985.
7. Ibid.
8. Ibid.
9. Ibid.
10. Bennis, Warren G., *On Becoming a Leader*, Reading, MA: Addison-Wesley, 1989.
11. Bennis, Warren G., "Managing the Dream: Leadership in the Twenty-First Century," *Journal of Organizational Change Management* 2 (no. 1), 1989.
12. Bennis, Warren G., and Biederman, Patricia Ward, *Organizing Genius: The Secrets of Creative Collaboration*, Reading, MA: Addison-Wesley, 1997.
13. Ibid.
14. Bennis, Warren G., and Heenan, David A., *Co-Leaders: The Power of Great Partnerships*, New York: John Wiley & Sons, 1999.
15. Bennis, Warren G., and Thomas, Robert J., *Geeks and Geezers: How Era, Values, and Defining Moments Shape Leaders*, Boston: Harvard Business School Press, 2002.

Chapter 3

1. Collins, James C., and Porras, Jerry I., *Built to Last: Successful Habits of Visionary Companies*, New York: HarperBusiness, 1994.

2. Ibid.

3. Ibid.

4. Collins, Jim, "Level 5 Leadership: The Triumph of Humility and Fierce Resolve," *Harvard Business Review*, January 2001.

5. Collins, Jim, "The Misguided Mix-up of Celebrity and Leadership," *Conference Board Annual Report*, September/ October 2001.

6. Collins, Jim, and Hansen, Morten T., *Great by Choice*, New York: HarperCollins, 2011.

Chapter 4

1. George, Bill, "Corporate Ethics: Where Have All the Leaders Gone?," Address to Westminster Town Hall Forum, 2003.

2. George, William W., *Authentic Leadership: Rediscovering the Secrets to Creating Lasting Value*, San Francisco: Jossey-Bass, 2003.

3. George, Bill, Sims, Peter, McLean, Andrew N., and Mayer, Diana, "Discovering Your Authentic Leadership," *Harvard Business Review*, February 2007.

4. Ibid.

5. Ibid.

6. Goffee, Robert, and Jones, Gareth, *The Character of a Corporation: How Your Company's Culture Can Make or Break Your Business*, New York: Harper Business, 1998.

7. Ibid.

8. Goffee, Rob, and Jones, Gareth, "Why Should Anyone Be Led by You?," *Harvard Business Review*, September– October 2000.

9. Goffee, Rob, and Jones, Gareth, "Authentic Leadership: Excite Others to Exceptional Performance," *Leadership Excellence*, issue 17, July 2009.

Chapter 5

1. Weber, Max, *On Charisma and Institution Building*, ed. S. N. Eisenstadt, Heritage of Sociology Series, Chicago: University of Chicago Press, 1968.
2. Khurana, Rakesh, "The Curse of the Superstar CEO," *Harvard Business Review*, September 2002.
3. Ibid.
4. Khurana, Rakesh, *Searching for a Corporate Savior: The Irrational Quest for Charismatic CEOs*, Princeton, NJ: Princeton University Press, 2004.
5. Conger, Jay, and Kanungo, Rabindra, *Charismatic Leadership in Organizations*, Thousand Oaks, CA: Sage, 1998.
6. Barbara Kellerman, *Bad Leadership: What It Is, How It Happens, Why It Matters*, Boston: Harvard Business School Press, 2004.
7. Finkelstein Sydney, *Why Smart Executives Fail and What You Can Learn from Their Mistakes*, New York: Portfolio, 2003.

Chapter 6

1. Follett, Mary Parker, *The Creative Experience*, New York: Longmans, Green, 1924.
2. Zaleznik, A., "The Dynamics of Subordinacy," *Harvard Business Review*, May–June 1965.
3. Gabarro, John, and Kotter, John, "Managing Your Boss," *Harvard Business Review*, 1980.
4. Ibid.
5. Ibid.
6. Kelley, R. E., "In Praise of Followers," *Harvard Business Review*, November 1988.
7. Ibid.
8. Kelley, R. E., *The Power of Followership: How to Create Leaders People Want to Follow and Followers Who Lead*

Themselves, New York: Doubleday/Currency, 1992; Kelley, R. E., "Rethinking Followership," in *The Art of Followership: How Great Followers Create Great Leaders and Organizations*, ed. R. E. Riggio, I. Chaleff, and J. Lipman-Blumen, San Francisco: Jossey-Bass, 2008.

9. Maccoby, Michael, "Why People Follow the Leader: The Power of Transference," *Harvard Business Review*, September 2004.

10. Ibarra, Herminia, *Working Identity: Unconventional Strategies for Reinventing Your Career*, Boston: Harvard Business School Press, 2003.

11. Ibarra, H., and Hunter, M., "How Leaders Create and Use Networks," *Harvard Business Review*, January 2007.

12. Ibarra, Herminia, and Hansen, Morten, "Are You a Collaborative Leader?," *Harvard Business Review*, July–August 2011.

13. Video: "Business Leaders," Thinkers50 interview after T50 awards, November 2011, www.herminiaibarra.com/p/videos-podcasts.html.

14. Ibarra, Herminia, "Leadership: Are You Connecting and Collaborating?," *INSEAD Knowledge*, July 2011.

15. Ibid.

16. Ibid.

17. "Business Leaders," Thinkers50 interview.

Chapter 7

1. Newman, Lee, "Rethinking Thinking Through Positive Leadership," www.iedp.com/Blog/Positive_Leadership.

2. Friedman, Stewart, *Great Leaders, Good Lives*, Boston: Harvard Business Review Press, 2014.

3. Friedman, Stewart, *Work and Family—Allies or Enemies?*, New York: Oxford University Press, 2000.

4. Friedman, Stewart, *Baby Bust*, Philadelphia: Wharton Digital Press, 2013.

Chapter 8

1. Hill, Linda A., "Becoming the Boss," *Harvard Business Review*, January 2007.
2. Hill, Linda A., and Lineback, Kent, "Are You a Good Boss—or a Great One?," *Harvard Business Review*, January 2011.
3. Radcliffe, Steve, *Leadership: Plain and Simple*, New York: FT Prentice Hall, 2010.
4. Ibid.

Acknowledgments

We would like to thank Steve Coomber for his help with this book. At the Thinkers50 we are grateful to our colleagues Joan Bigham and Deb Harrity for their essential and creative contributions. We would also like to thank all the people we have interviewed over the last 20 years writing about business thinking—in particular, Warren Bennis, Jim Collins, Rob Goffee, Marshall Goldsmith, Gareth Jones, Barbara Kellerman, Rakesh Khurana, Liz Mellon, and Kate Sweetman.

Index

About the Authors

Adjunct professors at IE Business School in Madrid, Stuart Crainer and Des Dearlove create and champion business ideas. They are the creators of Thinkers50 (www.thinkers50 .com), the original global ranking of business thought leaders. Their work in this area led *Management Today* to describe them as "market makers par excellence."

As journalists and commentators, Stuart and Des have been asking difficult questions for more than two decades. Now, they help leaders come up with their own wicked questions and explore how best to engage with people and communicate the answers. They were advisors to the 2009 British government report on employee engagement, and associates of the Management Innovation Lab at London Business School.

Their clients include Swarovski, the Department of Economic Development in Abu Dhabi, Fujitsu, and Heidrick & Struggles.

Stuart and Des have been columnists at the *Times* (London), contributing editors to the American magazine *Strategy+Business*, and edited the bestselling *Financial Times Handbook of Management*. Their books include *The Management Century*, *Gravy Training*, *The Future of Leadership*, and *Generation Entrepreneur*. These books are available in more than 20 languages.

Stuart is editor of *Business Strategy Review*. According to *Personnel Today*, he is one of the most influential figures in British people management. Des is an associate fellow of Saïd Business School at Oxford University and is the author of a bestselling study on the leadership style of Richard Branson.

Des and Stuart have taught MBA students, professors, and senior executives in programs all over the world. These include the Oxford Strategic Leadership Programme at the Saïd Business School at Oxford University; Columbia Business School in New York; the Tuck Business School at Dartmouth College in New Hampshire; IMD in Lausanne, Switzerland; and London Business School.

About the Thinkers50

The Thinkers50, the definitive global ranking of management thinkers, scans, ranks, and shares management ideas. It was the brainchild of Stuart Crainer and Des Dearlove, two business journalists, who identified a place in the market for an independent ranking of the top management thinkers. First published in 2001, the Thinkers50 has been published every two years since.

In 2011, Crainer and Dearlove added a number of award categories and hosted the first ever Thinkers50 Summit, described as "the Oscars of Management Thinking." The 2011 winner was Harvard Business School's Professor Clayton Christensen. The previous winners were C. K. Prahalad (2009 and 2007), Michael Porter (2005), and Peter Drucker (2003 and 2001).

The ranking is based on voting at the Thinkers50 website and input from a team of advisors led by Stuart Crainer and Des Dearlove. The Thinkers50 has 10 established criteria by which thinkers are evaluated:

- Originality of ideas
- Practicality of ideas
- Presentation style
- Written communication
- Loyalty of followers
- Business sense
- International outlook
- Rigor of research
- Impact of ideas
- Power to inspire

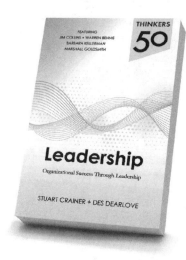